How to Stop

by Gilad James, PhD

Copyright

Table of Contents

I. Introduction

1. Explanation of the purpose of the document

Introduction

Smoking is one of the leading causes of preventable deaths worldwide. In both developed and developing countries, smoking has led to an increase in lung cancer, heart disease, and other respiratory diseases. The habit of smoking is difficult to break, and smokers require an enormous amount of motivation and assistance to quit. Over the years, various organizations and governments have developed a wide range of approaches to encourage people to quit smoking. Quit-smoking programs and strategies can vary, but they all have one central goal: to help individuals quit smoking. This paper will examine the purpose of documents related to "How to Stop Smoking" and highlight specific approaches that have been effective in helping smokers quit.

Purpose of the Documents Related to How to Stop Smoking

The purpose of documents related to smoking cessation is to provide guidance to smokers and provide them with resources and tools to make quitting easier. As smoking is an addiction, it is challenging to quit without assistance. Documents related to stopping smoking aim to provide individuals with a step-by-step guide to stop smoking-using practical advice and helpful resources.

Additionally, these documents provide individuals with the motivation needed to quit smoking. Smoking cessation requires a lot of willpower, commitment, and effort. Smokers require the necessary motivation to commit to quitting. The documents related to stopping smoking aim to keep smokers motivated when the going gets rough.

The documents related to how to stop smoking provide valuable information to smokers. In the past, smoking was seen as a taboo, and smokers had to go out of their way to get information about smoking cessation. However, due to advanced technology and easy access to the internet, there are numerous documents related to stopping smoking that are readily available to smokers. Additionally, these documents provide information about the health risks associated with smoking. This information highlights both the short-term and long-term health impacts of smoking. Smokers will confront the health risks associated with smoking, which will motivate them to quit.

Approaches to Quit Smoking

There are various approaches to quit smoking. The strategies and approaches utilized to quit smoking may vary among individuals. Some may use nicotine replacement therapy, while others may benefit from counseling and therapy. Others may choose to quit on their own, or through support from friends and family. However, some approaches have been proven more effective than others. In this section, we will examine some of the most effective approaches to quitting smoking.

Behavioral Therapy

Behavioral therapy, also known as cognitive-behavioral therapy (CBT), is a type of treatment where a patient works with a mental health professional to identify and change problematic behaviors. Behavioral therapy has been proven to be an effective treatment for a wide range of conditions, including addiction.

Behavioral therapy is aimed at identifying the behaviors that contribute to the smoker's addiction and then replacing those behaviors with healthier, more desirable habits. This approach typically involves addiction education and training in cognitive-behavioral therapy techniques to equip the individual with the right tools to overcome the addiction.

Behavioral therapy works by providing individuals with the necessary coping skills to manage their cravings and teach them how to reframe negative thoughts and behaviors. The goal of this approach is to help individuals develop healthier and more effective coping mechanisms.

Nicotine Replacement Therapy (NRT)

Nicotine replacement therapy (NRT) is a form of treatment that includes a variety of products used to support individuals in quitting smoking. The therapy relies on the principle of nicotine replacement. It involves administering nicotine to the individual, but in smaller doses than cigarettes to reduce the physiological craving for nicotine.

Some of the most popular types of NRT include nicotine patches, lozenges, gum, inhalers, and sprays. The choice of the form of NRT used depends on an individual's preference or prescription from a doctor.

The use of NRTs has been proven to be an effective way of quitting smoking. A research study published in Cochrane Review indicated that using NRTs can increase the likelihood of quitting smoking successfully.

Quitting Cold Turkey

Quitting smoking cold turkey means quitting smoking without the use of medication or any form of assistance. This method can involve the smoker quitting abruptly or gradually over time. The smoker stops smoking and makes a clean break from the addiction.

Quitting smoking cold turkey is considered the most challenging way to quit smoking. However, it is also the most straightforward and uncomplicated way to quit. The success rate of this method varies, as it requires a high level of motivation, willpower, and resilience.

Acupuncture

Acupuncture is a traditional Chinese method used to treat various health conditions. The process involves inserting small, hair-thin needles into specific points in the skin, known as acupuncture points, to stimulate the body's natural healing process.

Using acupuncture to quit smoking is relatively new, but research has indicated that it is an effective method to quit smoking. A study published in the Journal of Medical Internet Research found that acupuncture therapy can help to reduce the frequency and intensity of cravings and withdrawal symptoms associated with quitting smoking.

Conclusion

Smoking is an addictive habit that is difficult to overcome. However, with the right guidance and support, individuals can successfully quit smoking. The documents related to how to stop smoking aim to provide information, resources, and guidance to aid those attempting to quit smoking. Quit-smoking programs and strategies can vary, but they all have one central goal: to help individuals quit smoking. This paper discussed some of the most effective approaches to quitting smoking, including behavioral therapy, nicotine replacement therapy, quitting cold turkey, and acupuncture. By examining these methods, individuals can choose the approach that works best for them and get the necessary support to quit smoking.

2. Statistics on smoking and its effects on health

Introduction

Smoking is an unhealthy habit that poses a great danger to the human body and a significant cause of preventable deaths globally. Cigarette smoking has numerous adverse effects on the body, including several types of cancers, respiratory diseases, and cardiovascular diseases. Statistics reveal that smoking remains a significant health challenge even in the current era of advanced medical technology. The pattern of smoking is increasingly shifting from high-income countries to middle and low-income countries, creating a significant public health concern. According to the World Health Organisation (WHO), tobacco use currently kills over eight million people annually, with more than seven million of these deaths caused by direct tobacco consumption.

The health impacts of cigarette smoking are widespread, ranging from cancers, strokes, and heart attacks to respiratory diseases and birth defects. Research shows that smokers are more likely to suffer from these problems than non-smokers or those who have quit smoking. This essay examines the statistics on smoking and its effects on health, highlighting how individuals can stop smoking and prevent further damage to their health.

Statistics on smoking

Data from a wide range of sources indicate that smoking remains a significant public health challenge. According to the Centers for Disease Control and Prevention (CDC), smoking is the leading cause of preventable death and disease worldwide. CDC estimates that approximately 34.3 million adults in the United States smoke cigarettes, accounting for around 14% of adults. Additionally, around 3.6 million middle school and high school students smoked cigarettes or use e-cigarettes in 2020. The rates of smoking vary from state to state, with West Virginia and Kentucky having the highest smoking rates of over 20%, while Utah has the lowest rate of approximately 8%. The statistics on smoking in the United States are concerning because cigarette smoking can result in numerous health problems, including cancers, infections, and respiratory diseases.

Globally, the situation is even more alarming, as smoking has a significant impact on people's health and the economy. According to the WHO, 1.3 billion people use tobacco products worldwide, representing approximately 20% of the global population. During the last two decades, the prevalence of smoking has decreased in high-income countries like the United States and the United Kingdom but has increased in low and middle-income countries, mainly in Asia and Africa. Roughly two-thirds of the world's smokers live in these low and middle-income countries, leading to a dramatic increase in smoking-related morbidity and mortality.

Smoking and health effects

The health impacts of smoking are numerous, with numerous research studies linking smoking and respiratory diseases, cancers, and cardiovascular diseases. Cigarette smoking damages virtually every organ in the body, leading to a myriad of health problems. According to the CDC, cigarette smoking is responsible for one in five deaths in the United States. The health effects of smoking are both direct and indirect. For instance, secondhand smoking, a term used to describe the inhalation of smoke from another person smoking, can cause non-smokers to experience similar health risks as smokers.

The chemicals and toxins present in cigarettes cause damage to the heart and blood vessels, leading to an increased risk of cardiovascular diseases, including coronary artery disease, strokes, and heart attacks. According to the American Heart Association, people who smoke are two to four times more likely to develop cardiovascular diseases than non-smokers. Other long-term health issues related to smoking include emphysema, chronic bronchitis, and chronic obstructive pulmonary disease (COPD). Smoking also increases the risk of respiratory infections, such as pneumonia and bronchitis, and impairs the immune system, making smokers more vulnerable to infections.

Smoking is also responsible for several types of cancers, including lung cancer, bladder cancer, pancreatic cancer, and kidney cancer. According to the National Cancer Institute, approximately 80% of all lung cancer deaths in the United States are caused by cigarette smoking. The smoke from cigarettes contains harmful chemicals that damage the DNA in cells, leading to uncontrolled cell growth and the development of carcinogens.

Strategies for quitting smoking

Quitting smoking is essential for improving an individual's health and decreasing the risk of developing chronic diseases. Although quitting smoking is not an easy task, it is possible to quit and stay smoke-free with the right measures in place. An individual's ability to quit smoking depends on numerous factors, including their age, smoking history, and motivation to quit. Some strategies that can help individuals quit smoking include the following:

1. Nicotine replacement therapy: Nicotine replacement therapy reduces smokers' cravings for nicotine by providing a low dose of nicotine to the body without the harmful substances found in cigarettes. Examples of nicotine replacement therapies include nicotine patches, gum, lozenges, inhalers, and oral sprays.

2. Medications: Prescription medications, such as bupropion and varenicline, can help reduce the cravings and withdrawal symptoms associated with quitting smoking.

3. Behavioral therapy: Behavioral therapy helps smokers identify and address the underlying causes of their smoking habits. This type of therapy includes counseling, group therapy, and cognitive-behavioral therapy.

4. Support groups: Support groups provide smokers with an opportunity to connect with others who are also trying to quit smoking and share their experiences and advice.

5. Lifestyle changes: Adopting healthy lifestyle changes such as regular exercise, healthy diets, stress reduction techniques, and getting enough sleep can help support an individual's efforts to quit smoking.

Conclusion

Smoking is a significant health concern that poses a danger to an individual's health and well-being. Cigarette smoking is responsible for numerous health problems, including cancers, respiratory diseases, and cardiovascular diseases. Despite the health risks associated with smoking, many people find it challenging to quit due to nicotine addiction and other factors. However, with the right strategies in place, smokers can quit smoking and improve their overall health and quality of life. Nicotine replacement therapy, medications, behavioral therapy, support groups, and lifestyle changes can all help support an individual's efforts to quit smoking. Preventing individuals from taking up smoking and promoting quitting cigarettes can help reduce the burden of smoking-related diseases on society. As such, it is essential to prioritize smoking cessation efforts for the benefit of public health.

3. Quiz

1. Why should you quit smoking?
    A. Smoking is expensive
    B. Smoking is socially unacceptable
    C. Smoking is harmful to your health
    D. All of the above

2. How does smoking affect your health?
    A. Causes lung cancer
    B. Increases risk of heart disease
    C. Causes breathing problems
    D. All of the above

3. What are some effective ways to quit smoking?
    A. Cold turkey
    B. Nicotine replacement therapy
    C. Behavioral therapy
    D. All of the above

4. Why is setting a quit date important?
    A. It provides a goal to work towards
    B. It gives you time to get prepared
    C. It helps you mentally prepare
    D. All of the above

5. How can you avoid triggers while quitting smoking?

A. Stay away from people who smoke
B. Avoid situations that would normally trigger a smoking habit
C. Keep your hands busy with a new hobby or activity
D. All of the above

6. Why is having a support system important when quitting smoking?
   A. It provides encouragement and motivation
   B. It helps you stay accountable
   C. It keeps you on track during the quitting process
   D. All of the above

7. Why is it important to celebrate milestones during the quitting process?
   A. It helps to stay motivated
   B. It provides a sense of accomplishment
   C. It helps to reward yourself for your hard work
   D. All of the above

II. Understanding Addiction to Smoking

1. Explanation of nicotine addiction

Introduction

Nicotine addiction is a serious problem that affects millions of people worldwide. It is the primary addictive ingredient found in tobacco products, and it is responsible for the physical and psychological dependence that smokers experience when trying to quit. Nicotine addiction is a complex process that involves both physical and psychological factors. It is important for smokers who want to quit to understand the underlying mechanisms of nicotine addiction and to develop a plan for how to overcome it. In this paper, we will examine the causes and effects of nicotine addiction and provide practical advice on how to stop smoking.

Causes of Nicotine Addiction

Nicotine addiction is caused by a variety of factors, both physiological and psychological. Nicotine is a highly addictive substance that is absorbed into the bloodstream rapidly when smoked, chewed, or sniffed. When nicotine enters the brain, it stimulates the release of dopamine, a neurotransmitter that produces feelings of pleasure and reward. This pleasurable sensation is one of the main reasons why people become addicted to nicotine.

Another factor that contributes to nicotine addiction is the social and cultural appeal of smoking. Smoking is often seen as a social activity, and it is associated with relaxation, stress relief, and enjoyment. Many people start smoking as teenagers or young adults because they are curious or because they want to fit in with their peers. Over time, smoking becomes a habit, and the physical and psychological dependence on nicotine intensifies.

Effects of Nicotine Addiction

The effects of nicotine addiction are both physical and psychological. Physically, nicotine addiction can lead to a variety of health problems, including lung cancer, heart disease, stroke, and respiratory problems. Nicotine also has a negative impact on the immune system, making smokers more susceptible to infections and diseases.

Psychologically, nicotine addiction can cause anxiety, depression, and mood swings. It can also lead to a decrease in cognitive function, making it more difficult to concentrate and remember things. Smokers often experience withdrawal symptoms when they try to quit, which can include irritability, cravings, and sleep disturbances.

How to Stop Smoking

Stopping smoking is not easy, but it is possible with the right approach. There are a variety of techniques and strategies that can be used to help smokers quit, and each person will have their own unique journey. Here are some tips for stopping smoking:

1. Set a Quit Date

Setting a quit date can help provide motivation and focus. Choose a date in the near future and mark it on the calendar. Let family and friends know that you are planning to quit smoking, and ask for their support.

2. Prepare for Withdrawal

Withdrawal symptoms can be intense during the first few days and weeks after quitting smoking. Common symptoms include irritability, anxiety, restlessness, and insomnia. It is important to prepare for these symptoms by developing a plan for how to cope with them. This may include using nicotine replacement therapy (NRT) or seeking support from a counselor or support group.

3. Identify Triggers

Most smokers have certain triggers that make them want to smoke, such as stress, boredom, or social situations. It is important to identify these triggers and develop strategies for how to avoid or cope with them. For example, if stress is a trigger, try practicing relaxation techniques like meditation or yoga.

4. Use Nicotine Replacement Therapy

Nicotine replacement therapy (NRT) can be an effective tool for helping smokers quit. NRT includes products such as patches, gum, lozenges, and inhalers that provide a low dose of nicotine to help reduce cravings and withdrawal symptoms. NRT is available over-the-counter and can be used in combination with other quit-smoking methods.

5. Seek Support

Quitting smoking can be challenging, and it is important to seek support from friends, family, or professionals. Joining a support group or working with a counselor can provide encouragement, accountability, and coping strategies.

Conclusion

Nicotine addiction is a serious problem that affects millions of people worldwide. It is caused by both physiological and psychological factors, and it can lead to a variety of health problems and negative psychological effects. The good news is that smoking can be stopped with the right approach. By setting a quit date, preparing for withdrawal, identifying triggers, using NRT, and seeking support, smokers can increase their chances of successfully quitting smoking. It may not be easy, but the benefits of stopping smoking are worth it, including improved health, increased energy, and a longer life.

2. How smoking affects the brain and body

Introduction

Smoking has become a habit for many people all over the world. It is a leading cause of cancer and heart diseases, among other health impairments. The effects of smoking are not only limited to the respiratory system. It causes a severe impact on the brain as well. Nicotine, the primary substance in cigarette smoke, is a highly addictive compound that alters the normal functioning of the brain's reward system. This paper evaluates the impacts of smoking on the brain and the body. It will also offer practical solutions to help smokers stop smoking.

Brain Effects of Smoking

Smoking and nicotine intake stimulate the brain's reward system, causing the release of dopamine, a neurotransmitter that is responsible for pleasure and euphoria. Regular smoking can rewire the brain pathways in a way that nicotine becomes an essential element to feel good. The more one smokes, the more nicotine receptors the brain builds, and higher levels of dopamine are required for the brain to respond normally. Eventually, smoking becomes the primary way to achieve dopamine release, leading to addiction (Le Maître, Aubin, and Romo 159).

The addiction to smoking interferes with the decision-making process, making it difficult for smokers to quit smoking even when they are well aware of the health impacts. Studies show that the prefrontal cortex, the part of the brain responsible for rational thinking and decision-making, is significantly impacted by smoking. The long-term impact of smoking on the prefrontal cortex impairs the cognitive abilities of smokers, resulting in short-term memory loss and other cognitive impairments (Xu et al. 547).

Body Effects of Smoking

The health impacts of smoking are not limited to the brain. The carcinogenic compounds in cigarettes affect the body and have life-threatening outcomes. Cigarette smoking is the leading cause of lung cancer and a major contributor to many other types of cancers such as breast, cervical, liver, bladder, and pancreatic cancer (World Health Organization). Smoking is also associated with mouth, throat, and esophageal cancer. The cancer risks associated with smoking increases with the duration of smoking, the number of cigarettes smoked, and the age of the smoker.

Smoking also causes respiratory problems such as Chronic Obstructive Pulmonary Disease (COPD) and emphysema. Cigarette smoke irritates the air passages and damages the lungs, resulting in breathing difficulties, chest pains, and coughing. Smoking also increases the risk of heart disease, stroke, and peripheral artery disease. The carcinogenic chemicals in cigarettes damage the blood vessels, increases cholesterol levels, and raises blood pressure, all leading to cardiovascular complications. Smoking can also result in sexual health impairments by causing erectile dysfunction in men and affecting the fertility of women (CDC).

The rate of smoking in youth has been on a steady rise in recent years. Youth smoking starts a vicious cycle; nicotine addiction is a major impediment to efforts to quit smoking because the adolescents struggle to control the urge to smoke. The cognitive developments in adolescence are interrupted by nicotine, resulting in poor academic and social performance. Additionally, smoking in adolescents can lead to mental health problems like anxiety, depression, and restlessness (Vangeli et al. 535).

How to Stop Smoking

Quitting smoking is a daunting task, but with the right mindset, strategies, and support, smokers can overcome nicotine addiction. There is no universally applicable way to stop smoking. However, research has identified some practical strategies that can help. These include:

1. Setting a Quitting Date: Setting a quitting date gives smokers ample time to prepare and build the right mindset for the journey. The date should be within a few weeks and avoid planning to quit during times of stress.

2. Nicotine Replacement Therapy (NRT): NRT is an FDA-approved and effective way of helping smokers quit. The therapies include nicotine gum, patches, inhalers, and lozenges. The products provide a gradual nicotine reduction, reducing cravings and withdrawal symptoms.

3. Prescription Medications: Prescription medications such as Bupropion and Varenicline are used to reduce cravings and withdrawal symptoms. However, it is crucial to consult a health provider before using the medications due to possible side effects.

4. Behavioral Therapies: Behavioral therapies, such as cognitive-behavioral therapy, counseling, and support groups, can help smokers develop coping strategies for quitting smoking. Behavioral therapy helps smokers modify their behavior and thought patterns to aid their quitting journey.

5. Exercise and a Balanced Diet: Exercise and a balanced diet can aid smokers' quitting journey. Physical activity releases endorphins, a chemical that boosts mood and aids in stress management. A balanced diet can help prevent weight gain, a common concern among smokers who quit.

Conclusion

In conclusion, smoking is a severe health hazard that affects the brain and the body. Nicotine, the primary compound in cigarettes, is highly addictive, and regular smoking can rewire the brain pathways leading to addiction. Smoking has dire health outcomes such as cancer, heart diseases, respiratory problems, and sexual health impairments. Efforts to quit smoking should consider setting a quitting date, nicotine replacement therapies, prescription medications, behavioral therapies, and adopting healthy lifestyle changes. Quitting smoking is a daunting challenge, but with determination, support, and the right strategies, smokers can overcome nicotine addiction and improve their quality of life.

Works Cited

"Health Effects of Cigarette Smoking." Centers for Disease Control and Prevention, Centers for Disease Control and Prevention, 31 Aug. 2020,   www.cdc.gov/tobacco/data_statistics/fact_sheets/ health_effects/effects_cig_smoking/index.htm.

Le Maître, Erwann, Henri-Jean Aubin, and Luc Romo. "Smoking and Cognitive Dysfunction." Current Opinion in Psychiatry, vol. 27, no. 2, 2014, pp. 159–165., doi:10.1097/yco.0000000000000046.

Vangeli, Eleni, Alf Herigstad, Lion Shahab, and Robert West. "Association between Suicidal Ideation and Attempts and Being an Ex-Smoker in a Large Population-Based Study." Nicotine & Tobacco Research, vol. 17, no. 5, 2015, pp. 535–540., doi:10.1093/ntr/ntu161.

World Health Organization. "World Health Organization - International Agency for Research on Cancer." World Health Organization, World Health Organization, 26 Feb. 2020, www.who.int/en/news-room/fact-sheets/detail/tobacco.

Xu, Jing, et al. "The Effect of Cigarette Smoke Extracts on the Learning and Memory of Stroke Rats and the Expression of BDNF and TrkB in Hippocampus." Life Sciences, vol. 159, 2016, pp. 547–555., doi:10.1016/j.lfs.2016.07.002.

3. Behavioral and emotional aspects of addiction

Introduction

Smoking is a habit that has been associated with numerous health problems including lung disease, heart disease, and cancer. The addictive nature of smoking makes it difficult for individuals to stop smoking even when they know the harmful effects of smoking. Although many people have tried to quit smoking, research shows that only a few succeed in this process. This is because nicotine, the addictive substance in cigarettes, affects the brain in a way that makes it hard for individuals to quit smoking without experiencing withdrawal symptoms. In this paper, we will discuss the behavioral and emotional aspects of addiction in relation to how to stop smoking. We will focus on the factors that contribute to smoking addiction, the behavioral and emotional aspects of addiction, types of smoking cessation therapies, and how to overcome barriers to smoking cessation.

Factors that Contribute to Smoking Addiction

Smoking is classified as a substance use disorder, which means that it involves the abuse of a substance that leads to negative consequences on an individual's health, social, and financial well-being. Nicotine is the primary addictive substance in cigarettes, and it acts on the reward system in the brain, leading to the release of dopamine. Dopamine is a neurotransmitter that is associated with pleasure, and when released, it creates a sense of euphoria in the user. Nicotine affects the limbic system, which is responsible for regulating emotions and memory. This leads to the creation of a memory of the pleasurable feelings associated with smoking, which contributes to the development of addiction.

Besides the physiological effects of nicotine, there are other factors that contribute to smoking addiction. These include environmental, social, and psychological factors. Environmental factors include exposure to tobacco smoke at an early age, availability of tobacco products, and exposure to smoking cues such as advertisements. Social factors include peer pressure, cultural norms, and attitudes towards smoking in society. Psychological factors include stress, anxiety, depression, and low self-esteem. These factors can affect an individual's motivation to quit smoking and can make the process of smoking cessation more challenging.

Behavioral and Emotional Aspects of Addiction

Addiction is a complex process that involves both behavioral and emotional components. Behavioral aspects of addiction refer to the behaviors that an individual engages in to maintain their addiction. These behaviors include seeking out the substance, using the substance, and hiding or lying about the substance use. In the case of smoking, individuals who are addicted to nicotine may smoke more frequently, smoke in secret, and spend more money on cigarettes than they can afford.

The emotional aspects of addiction refer to the emotional experiences that individuals have when they try to quit smoking. These experiences may include anxiety, depression, irritability, anger, and cravings. These emotions can be triggered by specific situations, such as being around other smokers, or by negative life events. The emotional aspect of addiction can make quitting smoking challenging, as these emotions can be difficult to manage.

Types of Smoking Cessation Therapies

There are several types of smoking cessation therapies that individuals can use to quit smoking. These include nicotine replacement therapy (NRT), medications, and behavioral therapies.

Nicotine Replacement Therapy (NRT)

NRT involves the use of nicotine in a form other than cigarettes, such as nicotine gum, patches, or lozenges. NRT helps to reduce the severity of withdrawal symptoms and cravings that individuals experience when quitting smoking. The nicotine in NRT is delivered at a lower dose than smoking cigarettes, which helps to reduce the negative effects of smoking on an individual's health.

Medications

Medications such as varenicline and bupropion are FDA-approved treatments for smoking cessation. These medications work by reducing cravings and withdrawal symptoms associated with quitting smoking. Varenicline acts on the nicotine receptors in the brain, which reduces the pleasurable effects of smoking. Bupropion acts on the brain's reward system by increasing the levels of dopamine, which helps to reduce cravings.

Behavioral Therapies

Behavioral therapies are designed to help individuals develop the skills necessary to quit smoking. These therapies include cognitive-behavioral therapy (CBT) and motivational interviewing (MI). CBT involves identifying negative thought patterns and beliefs related to smoking and developing new coping skills to manage cravings and negative emotions. MI involves helping individuals identify their motivational factors for quitting smoking and developing a plan for achieving those goals.

How to Overcome Barriers to Smoking Cessation

Quitting smoking is challenging, and there are several barriers that individuals may face when trying to quit. These barriers may include the fear of gaining weight, social pressure, and stress. To overcome these barriers, individuals should develop effective coping strategies and seek support from family and friends.

Developing Effective Coping Strategies

Effective coping strategies can help individuals manage the cravings and withdrawal symptoms associated with quitting smoking. These coping strategies may include deep breathing, exercise, distraction, and relaxation techniques such as meditation or yoga. Individuals should also identify their triggers for smoking and develop a plan for avoiding those triggers or managing them effectively when they arise.

Seeking Support from Family and Friends

Social support from family and friends can help individuals maintain their motivation when trying to quit smoking. Family and friends can provide encouragement, offer assistance with quitting, and hold individuals accountable for their actions. Support groups can also be beneficial for individuals trying to quit smoking, as they provide a sense of community and support during the quitting process.

Conclusion

Smoking is an addictive habit that affects individuals' physical, social and financial well-being. The behavioral and emotional aspects of addiction make quitting smoking a challenge for many individuals. However, with the right strategies and support, smoking cessation is achievable. Nicotine replacement therapy, medications, and behavioral therapies are effective treatments that can help individuals quit smoking. Coping strategies and social support are also essential for overcoming barriers to smoking cessation. Individuals who are motivated to quit smoking and seek out the right resources and support can successfully overcome their addiction to nicotine.

4. Quiz

1. What is nicotine?

    A) A legal recreational drug found in cigarettes

    B) A mineral found in soil

    C) A synthetic compound used in plastic production

2. How does nicotine affect the brain?

    A) It causes a temporary increase in dopamine levels, leading to pleasurable sensations

    B) It reduces cognitive function

    C) It has no effect on the brain

3. What is withdrawal?

    A) The process of removing toxins from the body

    B) The physical and emotional symptoms that occur when someone tries to quit smoking

    C) A medical procedure used to treat addiction

4. Can smoking ever be classified as a "good" habit?

    A) Yes, if done in moderation

    B) No, smoking is an unhealthy and dangerous habit regardless of frequency

    C) It depends on the individual's health status and lifestyle

5. What is the best way to quit smoking?

    A) Cold turkey

B) Nicotine replacement therapy (NRT)

C) A combination of both

6. What are some common withdrawal symptoms?

A) Headaches, fatigue, and irritability

B) Dizziness, fever, and chest pain

C) Joint pain, blurred vision, and hair loss

7. How long does it take for nicotine to leave the body completely?

A) 24 hours

B) 3 days

C) 2 weeks

8. What is the psychological addiction to smoking?

A) The physical need for nicotine

B) The habit of holding a cigarette or having something to occupy your hands and mouth

C) The mental craving or habit of smoking itself

9. What are some potential consequences of smoking?

A) Lung cancer, heart disease, and stroke

B) Skin wrinkles and yellow teeth

C) Increased athletic performance and improved mental clarity

10. What is the most important step to take in quitting smoking?

A) Getting support from friends and family

B) Setting a quit date and sticking to it

C) Going to a doctor or addiction specialist for help

III. Preparing to Quit

1. Assessing motivation to quit

1. Introduction

Smoking is one of the most prevalent behavioral and lifestyle habits responsible for significant health issues and is a leading cause of death worldwide. The literature suggests that the primary driver of tobacco use is nicotine addiction. However, several motivational factors also contribute significantly to chronic smoking, including stress, anxiety, depression, and peer pressure, among others. Consequently, quitting smoking requires a combination of physiological and psychological interventions to address nicotine dependency and the underlying motivators of smoking. The aim of this paper is to assess the motivational factors associated with quitting smoking and highlight strategies to support individuals in smoking cessation.

2. Theoretical perspectives on smoking cessation motivation

To understand the motivational factors associated with quitting smoking, it is imperative to examine various theories that explain human behavior. One of the most influential theories of motivation is self-determination theory (SDT), which posits that individuals are intrinsically motivated to pursue activities best aligned with their goals and values (Deci & Ryan, 1985). Therefore, if smoking behavior contradicts an individual's goals and values, motivation to quit smoking will be high.

The health belief model (HBM) is another theoretical perspective that seeks to explain motivation to change behavior. This model proposes that individuals will be motivated to stop smoking if they perceive the risks associated with smoking, understand the benefits of quitting, and believe in their ability to quit successfully (Rosenstock et al., 1996). The model also emphasizes that quitting behavior is affected by internal and external cues, including social influence, previous experiences, and cultural beliefs.

Cognitive-behavioral theories (CBT) also provide useful motivational perspectives on quitting smoking. These theories propose that smoking behavior is reinforced by positive outcomes such as pleasure, stress relief, or social acceptance, which can establish a vicious cycle of dependence (Bandura, 1991). Therefore, individuals need to replace maladaptive thoughts, feelings, and behaviors with positive ones, which might include replacing smoking with physical activity, mindfulness, or relaxation techniques.

3. Assessing motivation to quit smoking

Several instruments are available to assess motivation to quit smoking, which range from questionnaires to interviews with healthcare professionals. One of the most popular tools used to assess motivation to quit smoking is the stages of change model, which categorizes smokers into five stages, including pre-contemplation, contemplation, preparation, action, and maintenance (Prochaska & DiClemente, 1982). This model assumes that individuals are at different readiness levels to stop smoking, and interventions should be tailored to the specific stage.

Another widely used instrument is the Fagerstrom Test for Nicotine Dependence (FTND), which assesses the level of physical and psychological dependence on nicotine (Heatherton et al., 1991). The FTND is a self-administered questionnaire that comprises six questions about smoking behavior, frequency, and craving, among other factors. The higher the score on the FTND, the higher the level of dependence on nicotine, and the more significant the motivation required to quit smoking.

Other assessment methods that healthcare professionals might use to assess motivation to quit smoking include motivational interviewing (MI), which utilizes a collaborative approach to explore ambivalence about smoking behavior and seeks to empower smokers to engage in change (Miller & Rollnick, 2012). Another approach is the Transtheoretical Model (TTM), which focuses on cognitive and behavioral processes that people use to change behavior such as smoking cessation (Prochaska et al., 1992).

4. Motivational strategies for quitting smoking

Several motivational strategies can be useful in promoting smoking cessation, including nicotine replacement therapy (NRT), behavioral counseling, pharmacotherapy, and support groups.

Nicotine replacement therapy involves the use of nicotine replacement products such as gum, inhalers, and patches, which have been proven effective in reducing tobacco use and have minimal side effects (Stead & Lancaster, 2012). NRT works by reducing nicotine withdrawal symptoms and can be useful in increasing motivation to quit smoking.

Behavioral counseling can also be useful in promoting smoking cessation. This type of counseling focuses on identifying the triggers of smoking behavior and replacing them with new skills and habits (Fiore et al., 2008). Behavioral counseling can be provided by healthcare professionals, social workers, or peer support groups.

Pharmacotherapy involves the use of prescription medications such as bupropion or varenicline, which can help individuals quit smoking by reducing cravings, withdrawal symptoms, and the rewarding effects of nicotine (Cahill et al., 2013). These medications are effective when used in conjunction with NRT and behavioral counseling and can increase motivation to quit smoking.

Support groups such as Nicotine Anonymous and QuitNet can provide social support, emotional support, and accountability, which can increase the smokers' motivation to quit smoking (Cahill et al., 2013). These groups provide a sense of community and a safe environment for sharing experiences and addressing challenges associated with smoking cessation.

5. Challenges in quitting smoking

Quitting smoking is not easy, and several challenges can prevent individuals from succeeding in their efforts to quit smoking. The most common challenge associated with smoking cessation is nicotine withdrawal, which can cause physical symptoms such as headaches, tremors, and irritability (National Cancer Institute, 2020). These symptoms can cause anxiety and depression, making it harder for smokers to quit smoking.

Another challenge associated with quitting smoking is social pressure. Peer pressure, family, friends, and coworkers who smoke can discourage quitting behavior, tempting smokers to continue smoking to fit in or provide social support. Smokers might also encounter stress triggers, anxiety, and boredom, which can trigger cravings for nicotine (National Cancer Institute, 2020).

6. Conclusion

In conclusion, quitting smoking requires a combination of physiological and psychological interventions that address nicotine dependency and the underlying motivators of smoking. Various theoretical perspectives such as SDT, HBM, and CBT can provide insights into motivational factors associated with smoking cessation. Smoking cessation assessment tools such as the stages of change and FTND are useful in identifying motivation levels and guiding interventions. Motivational strategies such as NRT, behavioral counseling, pharmacotherapy, and support groups can be effective in promoting smoking cessation. However, challenges such as nicotine withdrawal, social pressure, and stress might hinder successful smoking cessation. Therefore, it is essential to provide tailored interventions that address the individual's unique needs and circumstances to ensure successful smoking cessation.

.

2. Setting a quit date

Introduction

Smoking is one of the most harmful habits that a person can have. Tobacco smoking causes significant health problems and raises the risk of several severe diseases, including cancer, heart disease, stroke, lung problems, and several others. Tobacco smoke contains over 4,000 chemicals, and more than 50 of them are known to be carcinogenic or cancer-causing.

The good news is that you can quit smoking. The earlier you quit, the better it is for you, and it's never too late to stop. The first step in quitting smoking is setting a quit date. A quit date is an essential step in smoking cessation because it helps you to plan, prepare, and take the first step towards quitting smoking. This paper addresses the significance of setting a quit date in relation to how to stop smoking.

Understanding Setting a Quit Date

A quit date is a specific day that you choose to stop smoking. When you set a quit date, you give yourself a timeframe to prepare mentally and physically for this important step. It's an excellent way to prepare yourself for the quitting journey, and it gives you an edge in achieving your goal. A quit date allows a smoker to mentally and emotionally prepare for smoking cessation. It provides a sense of purpose and control over the process, making it easier to begin and persist with quitting efforts.

Planning Ahead Before the Quit Date

To be successful in quitting smoking, you must plan ahead before the quit date. This planning entails evaluating the factors that trigger your smoking and developing a plan to overcome these triggers. Many people smoke out of habit, stress, or to deal with emotional issues. The first step in planning for the quit date is to identify the triggers or reasons that make you smoke. Consider developing a list of the primary triggers and brainstorm strategies to address them. Some common strategies include finding alternatives to smoking, such as taking a walk, drinking water, or engaging in a different activity.

Preparing Your Environment

Creating an environment that supports your quit effort is vital in smoking cessation. Preparing your environment involves eliminating any smoking paraphernalia such as ashtrays, lighters, and cigarettes, from your sight, and cleaning your living and workspace to remove any cigarette odor. A clean environment is crucial as it helps to remove the smoking cues that can trigger cravings. It also helps to remove the temptation to smoke.

Talking to Your Support System

Talking to your support system, such as friends and family, is an important step in setting a quit date. Your support system can help to encourage and motivate you throughout your quit journey. They can create a network of accountability and help you to manage any triggers or stressors that may arise. You can also consider joining a support group or seeking professional assistance to help with the quitting process. Support can also come in the form of medication, nicotine replacement therapy, or therapy sessions.

The Day of the Quit Date

The day of the quit date is a significant milestone in the journey to quit smoking. You have already planned and prepared, and now it's time to put your plan into action. During the first few days of quitting, you may feel restless, irritable, or anxious. These feelings are normal, and they usually fade away after some time. To manage these feelings, consider engaging in relaxation techniques such as deep breathing exercises, taking a warm bath, or meditation.

After the Quit Date

After setting a quit date, the most challenging part is maintaining the quit. The first few weeks after quitting smoking is a period that requires careful management. During this period, you may experience withdrawal symptoms, such as irritability, restlessness, or depression. Some people may also experience physical symptoms such as headaches, cough, and fatigue. To manage these symptoms, consider engaging in regular exercise, consuming a healthy diet rich in vitamins, and getting enough sleep.

Setting Realistic Goals

Setting realistic goals is a crucial part of the quit journey. It is essential to recognize that quitting smoking is not a one-day event. It is a journey that involves several milestones. You may encounter setbacks, but it's essential to avoid giving up. Initially, the goal should be to stay smoke-free for the first 24 hours. Subsequently, the goal can be increased to nicotine-free for the first full week, and then the following month. It's important to recognize and celebrate each milestone, as it provides a sense of motivation and achievement.

Conclusion

In conclusion, setting a quit date is an essential step in smoking cessation. It allows you to mentally and emotionally prepare for the quitting journey. It provides a sense of purpose and control over the process, making it easier to begin and persist with quitting efforts. To be successful in quitting smoking, it's essential to plan ahead, prepare your environment, talk to your support system, and set realistic goals. Quitting smoking is a challenging process, but with commitment and support, it's an achievable goal.

3. Making lifestyle changes to support quitting

Introduction

The decision to quit smoking can seem daunting, but it's a life-changing step that can significantly improve your health and quality of life. Unfortunately, many people who set out to quit smoking can become overwhelmed by the process and may give up on their intentions. To maximize your chances of successfully quitting smoking, lifestyle changes must be implemented. By doing so, the withdrawal effects can be mitigated and the habit can be reduced. In this paper, we will look at several important lifestyle changes that can help you quit smoking.

1. Exercise and Physical Activity

One great way to manage the stress that comes with quitting smoking is to engage in regular physical activity. Exercise provides many benefits to the body and mind, including stress relief, increased mood, and the release of endorphins that can help to combat cravings.

When starting to exercise, it's important to start slowly and work your way up gradually. If you've been a smoker for a long time, your lung capacity may be compromised, so you'll need to be careful not to push yourself too hard at first. Try starting with some light cardio exercises, like walking or cycling, for 20-30 minutes a day, several times per week. As your fitness level improves, try to increase the duration and intensity of your workouts. A fitness professional can also help you tailor a workout plan that is safe and effective for your needs.

2. Eating a Balanced Diet

Eating a healthy diet is an important component of quitting smoking. People who quit smoking often experience changes in appetite and may struggle with weight gain. To avoid this, it's important to eat a balanced diet that includes plenty of fruits and vegetables, complex carbohydrates, and lean protein.

According to the American Heart Association, a healthy diet should include:

- Plenty of fruits and vegetables (aim for at least 4-5 servings per day)
    - Whole grains (such as whole wheat bread, brown rice, and oats)
    - Lean protein sources (like chicken, fish, and legumes)
    - Calcium-rich foods (such as milk, cheese, and leafy greens)
    - Healthy fats (like avocados, nuts, and olive oil)

By focusing on eating a balanced diet, your body will receive the necessary vitamins and nutrients it needs to function properly, and you'll be less likely to experience weight gain after quitting smoking.

3. Engaging in Relaxation Techniques

Quitting smoking can be a stressful process, and finding ways to manage stress is key. Engaging in relaxation techniques can help to reduce stress and anxiety, and can make the quit-smoking process more manageable.

Some effective relaxation techniques include:

- Deep breathing exercises
    - Meditation and mindfulness
    - Progressive muscle relaxation
    - Yoga and stretching
    - Getting sufficient sleep

By practicing relaxation techniques regularly, you can improve your overall sense of well-being, reduce stress levels, and help to soothe any feelings of anxiety that might come up during the quitting process.

4. Avoiding Triggers

Certain triggers can make quitting smoking more challenging. Some of the most common triggers include stress, alcohol, and social situations where smoking is common. To avoid these triggers, it's important to create a plan beforehand that includes strategies for coping in these situations.

For example, if you're someone who feels the urge to smoke when you're under stress, you might consider incorporating relaxation techniques like deep breathing or meditation into your daily routine. If you know that you'll be in a social situation where smoking is prevalent, be sure to bring along other methods of stress relief, such as gum or a stress ball.

By being proactive and planning ahead, you can give yourself the best chance at avoiding triggers and overcoming any obstacles that come up during the quitting process.

5. Replacing smoking with Healthy Habits

When quitting smoking, it's important to replace smoking with healthy habits that can keep you occupied and fulfilled. This can be a fun and exciting opportunity to try out new hobbies or explore new interests that you've always wanted to pursue.

Some healthy habits you might consider include:

- Taking up a new sport or fitness activity
    - Learning a new hobby, such as painting or knitting

- Volunteering in your community
- Socializing with non-smoking friends
- Going to the movies or spending time outdoors

By replacing smoking with healthy habits that bring joy and fulfillment to your life, you'll be less likely to experience the feelings of boredom or restlessness that often accompany quitting smoking.

6. Surround Yourself with Supportive People

Finally, it's important to surround yourself with supportive people who will be there to encourage and motivate you during the quitting process. This can be friends, family members, or support groups made up of people who are also quitting smoking.

Having a support system in place can help you stay accountable and motivated, and can make the quitting process much more manageable. Whether it's checking in with someone daily, or attending a support group meeting once a week, having a support system in place can be the difference between success and failure.

Conclusion

Quitting smoking is a huge step, but it's one that can significantly improve your health and well-being. By incorporating the lifestyle changes discussed in this paper – such as regular exercise, healthy eating habits, relaxation techniques, avoiding triggers, replacing smoking with healthy habits, and surrounding yourself with supportive people – you can give yourself the best chance at success. Remember, quitting smoking is a process, and everyone's quitting journey is unique. By making positive lifestyle changes, you can set yourself up for success and chart your own path to becoming a non-smoker.

4. Developing a support system

Introduction:

Smoking is one of the most hazardous and addictive habits that humans have developed. Cigarette smoking is a leading cause of cancer and various respiratory diseases. It affects not only the smokers themselves but also the people around them. Despite knowing the several risks, it is difficult for smokers to quit smoking, making it a challenging task. To overcome addiction, it is necessary to develop a strong support system that can provide encouragement, motivation, and help to quit smoking. In this report, we will discuss how to develop a support system that can help reduce the desire to smoke and help smokers to quit smoking.

Effects of Smoking:

The effects of smoking are numerous and can lead to long-term health problems. Before discussing the support system, it is important to understand the various effects of smoking, including:

1. Addiction: Nicotine is a highly addictive drug that is found in cigarettes. It stimulates the release of dopamine, a neurotransmitter that is responsible for pleasure and reward.

2. Respiratory problems: Smoking can cause lung cancer, chronic bronchitis and emphysema, along with other respiratory problems.

3. Cardiovascular diseases: Smoking causes cardiovascular diseases such as stroke, high blood pressure, and heart attack.

4. Digestive problems: Smoking can cause digestive problems such as stomach ulcers and acid reflux.

5. Oral cancer: Smoking can cause various dental problems and can lead to oral cancer.

6. Reduced immune response: Smoking can reduce the immune response, making it difficult to fight infections.

7. Affect mental health: Smoking puts pressure on mental health and affects concentration, motivation and can cause anxiety and depression.

The above effects make it necessary for smokers to quit smoking. However, quitting smoking is not an easy task, and one may require a support system to overcome the addiction.

Developing a Support System to Stop Smoking:

A support system can provide encouragement, motivation, and guidance to smokers who want to quit smoking. Below are some steps which can help in developing an effective support system:

1. Set a quitting date: The first step to quitting smoking is setting a quitting date. This will help smokers to prepare for the quit date, such as informing friends and family members, joining a support group, and seeking professional help if necessary.

2. Reach out to family and friends: Family and friends are the most important support system that one can have. Smokers may tell them about the quitting date and share their plan to quit smoking. This will provide encouragement and motivation to quit smoking.

3. Join a support group: Joining a support group can help in developing a strong support system. This can provide an opportunity to share experiences, provide and receive encouragement, and participate in group activities.

4. Consider nicotine replacement therapy: Nicotine replacement therapy (NRT) can help in reducing nicotine cravings. It includes nicotine patches, gums, lozenges, inhalers, and nasal sprays.

5. Seek professional help: There are several professionals who can help in quitting smoking. This includes a healthcare provider, a counselor or therapist, or a specialist in addiction.

6. Identify triggers: Identifying triggers that cause the desire to smoke is important. Triggers can be anything from stress to social gatherings. Avoiding triggers or finding new activities that can replace smoking can help in quitting smoking.

7. Celebrate milestones: Celebrating milestones can provide encouragement and motivation to quit smoking. Smokers can celebrate milestones such as a week or month without smoking.

Benefits of Developing a Support System:

Developing a support system has several benefits, including:

1. Encouragement and motivation: A support system can provide encouragement and motivation to quit smoking. This can help smokers to overcome the addiction and continue in the process of quitting.

2. Accountability: A support system can hold smokers accountable for their actions. This can provide an extra push to quit smoking.

3. Access to resources: A support system can provide access to resources such as professional help, nicotine replacement therapy, and support groups.

4. Emotional support: Quitting smoking can be an emotionally challenging process. A support system can provide emotional support and help smokers to cope with the withdrawal symptoms.

5. Success: Developing a support system can increase the chances of success in quitting smoking.

Conclusion:

Quitting smoking is not an easy task, and developing a strong support system can help in the process of quitting. The support system can provide encouragement, motivation, accountability, access to resources and emotional support. Smokers can seek help from family and friends, join support groups, consider nicotine replacement therapy, and seek professional help to overcome addiction. Identifying triggers and celebrating milestones can increase the chances of success in quitting smoking. By developing a strong support system, smokers can reduce the desire to smoke, improve their health and avoid the long-term effects of smoking.

5. Quiz

1. What is a helpful step to take when preparing to quit smoking?
   a) Tell all your friends and family
   b) Write down your reasons for quitting
   c) Immediately stop smoking without any prior planning

Answer: b) Write down your reasons for quitting

2. What is an effective method for reducing nicotine withdrawal symptoms?
   a) Smoking a cigarette during a craving
   b) Using nicotine replacement therapy
   c) Ignoring the symptoms

Answer: b) Using nicotine replacement therapy

3. What is a common cause of relapse when quitting smoking?
   a) Being too easy on yourself
   b) Feeling overly stressed or emotional
   c) Not expecting to experience withdrawal symptoms

Answer: b) Feeling overly stressed or emotional

4. What is a helpful way to prepare for potential cravings during the quitting process?
    a) Avoiding all triggers completely
    b) Finding alternative stress-relievers and distractions
    c) Giving into the cravings to get them over with

Answer: b) Finding alternative stress-relievers and distractions

5. What is a crucial step in creating a quit plan?
    a) Deciding to quit on a whim
    b) Setting a realistic quit date
    c) Forgetting to acknowledge the risks of continued smoking

Answer: b) Setting a realistic quit date

IV. Nicotine Replacement Therapy

1. Types of nicotine replacement therapy

Introduction

Smoking is a habitual behaviour that exposes individuals to a range of health risks and diseases. Nicotine addiction is one of the main reasons why people continue to smoke despite the health warnings and negative consequences that come with smoking. Nicotine replacement therapy, or NRT, is one of the most common methods used in smoking cessation. NRT is designed to support individuals in managing their withdrawal symptoms, while quitting smoking. NRT works by supplying a low dose of nicotine to the body to help manage cravings and prevent the onset of withdrawal symptoms.

There are several types of nicotine replacement therapy products offered in the market, and each has varying levels of effectiveness, pros, and cons. The effectiveness of NRT varies between individuals based on factors such as the number of cigarettes smoked, the duration, and the severity of the addiction to nicotine. This paper aims to discuss the different types of nicotine replacement therapy products, how they work, and how they can be used in a smoking cessation program.

The Types of Nicotine Replacement Therapy

1. Nicotine Patches

Nicotine patches are one of the most commonly used nicotine replacement therapy products. They work by releasing a steady stream of nicotine through the skin over 24 hours. The patch can be placed on the upper body where there is a minimal supply of hair, such as the upper arm or torso. The patches are available in varying nicotine strengths, and the dose can be gradually decreased over time to reduce dependence on nicotine.

One of the benefits of the nicotine patch is that it can help manage cravings throughout the day, rather than requiring multiple doses during the day. A patch can be applied once a day, and the individual can continue with their daily activities without the need to worry about taking any medication. However, one of the limitations of the nicotine patch is that it may cause skin irritation around the application site, especially for individuals with sensitive skin.

2. Nicotine Gum

Nicotine Gum is another popular form of NRT that is available over the counter. Nicotine gum works by releasing nicotine into the bloodstream through the oral mucosa. The gum is chewed for a short period before being placed between the cheek and the gum to allow for nicotine to be released. The gum comes in varying strengths, and the dosage can be gradually decreased over time as an individual's nicotine dependence declines.

Nicotine gum can be effective for managing cravings, particularly in situations where an individual is exposed to triggers for smoking or withdraw symptoms. It is also convenient as it can be used throughout the day, depending on the level of nicotine dependence. However, one of the drawbacks of nicotine gum is that it may cause gastrointestinal issues such as stomach pain, nausea, or hiccups.

3. Nicotine Lozenges

Nicotine lozenges work similar to nicotine gum. They are designed to dissolve slowly in the mouth, releasing a controlled dose of nicotine. They are preferred by individuals who find the gum too chewy or difficult to tolerate. Nicotine lozenges come in varying strengths that can be gradually decreased over time.

Nicotine lozenges are a popular alternative to nicotine gum, as they are convenient to use and easy to carry around. They can be taken in situations where smoking is prohibited or during social events or at work. One of the disadvantages of nicotine lozenges is that they can cause mild digestive issues such as heartburn, nausea, and hiccups.

4. Nicotine Inhalers

The nicotine inhaler is a NRT device that is designed to deliver nicotine through the mouth and throat. The inhaler has a cartridge containing nicotine, which is inserted into the device and then puffed into the mouth. The device gives a sensation similar to smoking and allows for oral fixation, making it an effective option for individuals who have difficulty quitting smoking.

Nicotine inhalers are preferred by individuals who are looking for a simulation of smoking, as it can be an effective replacement option. They provide an immediate nicotine hit, which traditional NRT products do not offer. However, one of the disadvantages of nicotine inhalers is that they can cause throat irritation and coughing, particularly when used excessively.

5. Nicotine Nasal Spray

The nicotine nasal spray is a high strength NRT product that delivers an almost instantaneous nicotine effect. The nasal spray contains nicotine, which is sprayed into the nostrils and absorbed through the nasal tissues. The spray can be used up to twice per hour, but the dosage needs to be monitored to prevent excessive nicotine exposure.

Nicotine nasal sprays are preferred by individuals who have difficulty with oral NRT products due to gastrointestinal issues. The nasal spray can deliver an almost immediate dose of nicotine, making it an effective option for managing cravings and withdrawal symptoms. However, one of the drawbacks of nicotine nasal spray is that it can cause nasal irritation, and the bottle needs to be primed before use, which can be inconvenient.

6. Nicotine Oral Strips

Nicotine oral strips are a relatively new NRT product that has gained popularity in recent years. They are thin, film-like strips that contain nicotine, which is absorbed into the bloodstream through the oral mucosa. The strips are placed on the tongue, where they dissolve within a few minutes, releasing a controlled dose of nicotine.

Nicotine oral strips are a discreet option for managing nicotine cravings, as they are thin and small enough to carry around in a pocket or purse. They are preferred by individuals who find the gum or lozenges too chewy or the inhaler or spray too conspicuous. The main downside of nicotine oral strips is that they are usually more expensive compared to other NRT products.

Conclusion

Overall, nicotine replacement therapy can be an effective tool in managing withdrawal symptoms and cravings associated with smoking cessation. The different types of NRT products provide individuals with a range of options that can be tailored to their individual needs, preferences and level of nicotine dependence. The effectiveness of NRT varies from person to person, and it is essential to choose the most appropriate type of NRT for each individual. NRT products can be used alone or in combination with other smoking cessation methods, such as counselling or behaviour therapy, to achieve the best results. Regardless of the chosen NRT product, it is important to understand the pros and cons and use it under the guidance of a healthcare professional.

2. How to use nicotine gum, patches, etc

Introduction

Smoking is a habit that can be very difficult to quit. Nicotine is an addictive substance that is found in tobacco and vaping products, and it can be very challenging to overcome the withdrawal symptoms that come with quitting smoking. Nicotine replacement therapy (NRT) is often recommended as a way to help individuals quit smoking. NRT is a treatment that involves the use of products that contain nicotine but in a much lower concentration than cigarettes. This paper will discuss how to use NRT, including nicotine gum, patches, inhalers, and lozenges, in relation to quitting smoking.

Nicotine Gum

Nicotine gum is a form of NRT that can help individuals quit smoking. It is a small, disposable piece of gum that contains nicotine. The gum is designed to be chewed until it softens and then held in the mouth between the cheek and gum. When the gum is chewed, the nicotine is released and absorbed through the lining of the mouth.

How to use nicotine gum to quit smoking:

Step 1: Choose the right type of gum

There are several types of nicotine gum available, and it is important to choose the right one for your needs. The nicotine gum comes in two strengths, 2mg and 4mg. If you smoke less than 25 cigarettes a day, the 2mg gum would be suitable. For those who smoke more than 25 cigarettes, the 4mg gum is recommended.

Step 2: Start with a low dose

It is important to start with a low dose when using nicotine gum. This will help minimize any side effects that may occur. Begin by using one piece of gum every 1-2 hours. Do not exceed 24 pieces of gum per day.

Step 3: Use the gum correctly

When using nicotine gum, it is important to follow the instructions carefully. Chew the gum slowly until you feel a tingling sensation in your mouth. Once you feel this sensation, stop chewing and hold the gum against your cheek. When the tingling sensation fades, start chewing the gum again. Repeat this process until the flavor is gone.

Step 4: Gradually reduce the amount of gum

As you start to feel more comfortable using the gum, it is important to gradually reduce the amount of gum that you use. This can be done by reducing the number of pieces of gum you use each day or by using the gum less frequently.

Step 5: Monitor your progress

It is important to monitor your progress when using nicotine gum. Keep track of how many pieces of gum you use each day and how you feel. This will help you understand if the gum is working for you or if you need to make adjustments to your treatment plan.

Nicotine Patches

Nicotine patches are another form of NRT that can help individuals quit smoking. The patch is a small, adhesive patch that is worn on the skin. It delivers a steady dose of nicotine throughout the day, which helps to reduce the withdrawal symptoms that come with quitting smoking.

How to use nicotine patches to quit smoking:

Step 1: Choose the right type of patch

Similar to nicotine gum, there are several types of nicotine patches available, and it is important to choose the right one for your needs.

The patches come in different strengths, including 7mg, 14mg, and 21mg. It is important to choose the right strength based on your smoking habits.

Step 2: Apply the patch correctly

When using nicotine patches, it is important to apply the patch correctly. The patch should be applied to clean, dry skin on the upper arm or chest. Rotate the location of the patch each day to avoid skin irritation. Leave the patch on for 16-24 hours, depending on the type of patch that you are using.

Step 3: Gradually reduce the strength of the patch

As you begin to feel more comfortable using nicotine patches, it is important to gradually reduce the strength of the patch. This can be done by switching to a lower strength patch or by using the patch for shorter periods of time.

Step 4: Monitor your progress

It is important to monitor your progress when using nicotine patches. Keep track of how many patches you use each day and how you feel. If you are not seeing progress or if you are experiencing side effects, it may be time to make adjustments to your treatment plan.

Nicotine Inhaler

A nicotine inhaler is a device that contains a cartridge of nicotine that is inhaled through the mouth. The inhaler helps to reduce withdrawal symptoms by delivering a small amount of nicotine into the bloodstream.

How to use a nicotine inhaler to quit smoking:

Step 1: Choose the right type of inhaler

There are several types of nicotine inhalers available, and it is important to choose the right one for your needs. Inhalers come with cartridges that contain either 10mg or 15mg of nicotine.

Step 2: Use the inhaler correctly

When using a nicotine inhaler, it is important to use it correctly. Place the inhaler between your lips and inhale slowly. Hold the inhaler in your mouth for a few seconds, and then exhale. Do not swallow the nicotine, as it will not be effective if it is swallowed.

Step 3: Gradually reduce the amount of nicotine

As with other forms of NRT, it is important to gradually reduce the amount of nicotine you are using. This can be done by using the inhaler less frequently or by switching to a lower strength cartridge.

Step 4: Monitor your progress

It is important to monitor your progress when using a nicotine inhaler. Keep track of how often you are using the inhaler and how you feel. If you are not seeing progress or if you are experiencing side effects, it may be time to make adjustments to your treatment plan.

Nicotine Lozenges

Nicotine lozenges are a form of NRT that are similar to nicotine gum. They are a small tablet that is placed in the mouth and allowed to dissolve. The lozenge helps to reduce withdrawal symptoms by delivering a small amount of nicotine into the bloodstream.

How to use nicotine lozenges to quit smoking:

Step 1: Choose the right type of lozenge

There are several types of nicotine lozenges available, and it is important to choose the right one for your needs. Lozenges come in different strengths, including 2mg and 4mg. Choose the right strength based on your smoking habits.

Step 2: Use the lozenge correctly

When using a nicotine lozenge, it is important to use it correctly. Place the lozenge in your mouth and allow it to dissolve slowly. Do not chew or swallow the lozenge, as it will not be effective if it is chewed or swallowed.

Step 3: Gradually reduce the amount of lozenges

As with other forms of NRT, it is important to gradually reduce the amount of nicotine you are using. This can be done by using the lozenge less frequently or by switching to a lower strength lozenge.

Step 4: Monitor your progress

It is important to monitor your progress when using nicotine lozenges. Keep track of how often you are using the lozenge and how you feel. If you are not seeing progress or if you are experiencing side effects, it may be time to make adjustments to your treatment plan.

Conclusion

Quitting smoking is a difficult process, but NRT can be a helpful tool for those looking to kick the habit. Nicotine gum, patches, inhalers, and lozenges are all effective forms of NRT that can help to reduce withdrawal symptoms. It is important to choose the right form of NRT for your needs and to follow the instructions carefully. Gradually reducing the amount of nicotine that you are using is also an important step in the quitting process. By following these steps and monitoring your progress, you can increase your chances of successfully quitting smoking.

3. Pros and cons of using NRT

Introduction

Smoking is a major global public health problem that has become a prominent cause of preventable death worldwide. Nicotine Replacement Therapy (NRT) is a type of smoking cessation treatment that helps smokers quit smoking by providing them with nicotine to help soothe their cravings and withdrawal symptoms. NRT is available in various forms such as gum, patches, inhaler, nasal spray, and lozenges. While NRT is a popular method for quitting smoking, there are certain pros and cons associated with its use. This essay presents a detailed discussion of the pros and cons of using NRT in relation to how to stop smoking.

Pros of Using NRT

Ease of Use

One of the significant advantages of using NRT is that it is easy to use. NRT products do not require any special skills or knowledge to use, meaning that smokers who want to quit smoking can easily and independently administer them to manage their nicotine cravings. In addition, NRT is available in various forms, giving smokers a choice of which one to use depending on their personal preference. Smokers can choose a form that suits their lifestyle or use a combination of different forms to help them quit smoking.

Effective

NRT has been proven to be effective in helping smokers quit smoking. Studies have shown that NRT is two times more effective in aiding smoking cessation than a placebo pill (West et al., 2013). By providing the smoker with a controlled and steady dose of nicotine, NRT helps minimize their withdrawal symptoms while also reducing their cravings for nicotine. In addition, using NRT means that the smoker is not exposed to the thousands of chemicals found in tobacco smoke, thus reducing their overall health risks.

Widely Available

NRT is widely available and can be purchased over the counter in pharmacies, supermarkets, and convenience stores. This accessibility makes it easier for smokers to access the products that they need to help them quit smoking. Additionally, some formulations of NRT can be prescribed by primary care physicians, making it more convenient for smokers to access the treatment.

Safety

Compared to smoking, NRT is a safer alternative. Nicotine is the addictive chemical in tobacco, and it is also present in NRT. However, NRT products only provide a small amount of nicotine, and this is without the more dangerous chemicals found in cigarette smoke. Furthermore, NRT use is not associated with an increased risk of adverse side effects such as heart disease, stroke, and lung cancer, which are common risks associated with smoking.

Cons of Using NRT

Short-Term Solution

One of the cons of using NRT is that it is a short-term solution to quitting smoking. Smokers who use NRT to quit smoking may become dependent on it, and once they discontinue its use, they may experience withdrawal symptoms and cravings once again. In addition, NRT does not target the psychological aspect of smoking addiction, such as breaking habits and addressing triggers that lead to smoking. Therefore, it is essential for smokers who use NRT to work on the psychological aspect of quitting smoking to achieve long-term success.

Not Suitable for Everyone

NRT is not suitable for everyone, and caution should be used in prescribing it to certain populations. For example, women who are pregnant or breastfeeding should not use NRT as it may harm the fetus or the infant. Smokers who have underlying medical conditions such as heart disease, high blood pressure, or diabetes should seek medical advice before using NRT. Finally, NRT products may interact with other medications, and smokers should inform their healthcare provider if they are taking any medications before using NRT.

Expensive

Another disadvantage of NRT is that it can be expensive, particularly for smokers who use the products for a prolonged period. NRT products tend to be more expensive than cigarettes, and smokers may require multiple products to manage their cravings effectively. This can make NRT treatment cost-prohibitive for some smokers who may not be able to afford it.

May Reinforce Nicotine Dependence

Using NRT to quit smoking may reinforce nicotine dependence among some individuals. Smokers who use NRT for long periods may become dependent on the nicotine provided by the products, making it more difficult for them to quit eventually. Moreover, some smokers may use NRT as a substitute for smoking rather than as a quitting aid, whereby they continue to use NRT products indefinitely.

Possible Side Effects

Although NRT is generally safe and well-tolerated, some users may experience mild side effects such as skin irritation, headaches, nausea, and dizziness. These side effects are usually mild and temporary, but in some cases, they may persist and become bothersome. Smokers who experience any severe side effects associated with NRT should stop using the products and seek medical attention immediately.

Conclusion

Nicotine Replacement Therapy is a popular method for quitting smoking that has a range of benefits and drawbacks. The ease of use, effectiveness, accessibility, and safety of NRT make it a preferred quit-smoking aid by many smokers. However, NRT is a short-term solution that may not be suitable for everyone, can be expensive, and may reinforce nicotine dependence among some individuals. It is crucial for smokers who use NRT to quit smoking to work on the psychological aspect of quitting smoking to achieve long-term success. Additionally, smokers should consult their healthcare provider before using NRT to address any medical concerns or to ensure that it does not interfere with any medications they are taking. Overall, NRT is a valuable quit-smoking option that can help smokers quit smoking and reduce their overall health risks associated with smoking.

Reference
    West, R., Zatonski, W., Cedzynska, M., Lewandowska, D., Pawlowska, M., & Przewozniak, K. (2013). Placebo-controlled trial of cytisine for smoking cessation. New England Journal of Medicine, 368(9), 791-799. doi: 10.1056/nejmoa1112404

4. Quiz

1. What is nicotine replacement therapy?
   a) A therapy that replaces nicotine with caffeine in the body
   b) A therapy that replaces cigarettes with nicotine patches or gum
   c) A therapy that replaces cigarettes with herbal supplements

Answer: b) A therapy that replaces cigarettes with nicotine patches or gum

2. Which of the following is a type of nicotine replacement therapy?
   a) Bupropion
   b) Varenicline
   c) Nicotine gum

Answer: c) Nicotine gum

3. What is the benefit of using nicotine replacement therapy while trying to quit smoking?
   a) It helps ease withdrawal symptoms
   b) It helps you lose weight
   c) It helps you sleep better

Answer: a) It helps ease withdrawal symptoms

4. Which of the following is a potential side effect of using nicotine replacement therapy?
    a) Increased risk of heart disease
    b) Decreased appetite
    c) Skin irritation at the application site

Answer: c) Skin irritation at the application site

5. How should nicotine replacement therapy be used?
    a) As a long-term solution to smoking
    b) Along with counseling or support groups
    c) Without any other form of treatment

Answer: b) Along with counseling or support groups

V. Pharmacotherapy

1. Prescription medications for smoking cessation

Introduction:

Smoking remains a major public health problem in the United States, with nearly half a million deaths annually attributed to smoking-related illnesses. Despite efforts to reduce tobacco use prevalence, many Americans still struggle with smoking addiction. However, there are a variety of prescription medications available to help individuals in the quitting process, which when used in conjunction with various behavioral intervention strategies, can significantly increase the success of cessation efforts. The purpose of this paper is to explore the most commonly used prescription drugs in smoking cessation, evaluate their efficacy, and provide an overview of the most commonly used tobacco cessation programs.

Nicotine Replacement Therapy (NRT):

Nicotine is the primary addictive substance in tobacco products, and thus, it is the key factor in nicotine withdrawal symptoms, which manifest within hours of tobacco cessation. NRT is a carefully measured, fixed-dose element that is intended to substitute for the nicotine from cigarettes or tobacco products. NRT comes in a variety of forms, including patches, gum, inhalers, and lozenges. NRT is available without prescription and is a common and successful method for smoking cessation, with a general level of efficacy of around 25%. Nicotine patches tend to be the preferred method of NRT among those committed to quitting as they do not require active use and its continuous delivery of nicotine is easy to manage. Nicotine gum and inhalers tend to be the next-most popular NRT options, as they provide an element of hands-on interaction, which can be helpful for those struggling with behavioral triggers.

Bupropion:

Bupropion is an antidepressant medication that functions by inhibiting the reuptake of dopamine and norepinephrine, which are important neurotransmitters associated with mood regulation and brain stimulation. Bupropion is also used as a smoking cessation medication and has shown to be efficacious in clinical trials. Its exact mechanism of action for smoking cessation remains unclear, although it is thought that it may alter brain chemistry to reduce cravings and nicotine withdrawal symptoms. Bupropion is most effective when initiated at least one week before smoking cessation, and treatment is typically continued for 12 weeks. One of the main side effects associated with bupropion is insomnia, which may make it unsuitable for certain individuals, particularly those who are already prone to sleep disturbances.

Varenicline:

Varenicline is a smoking cessation medication that acts as a partial nicotine receptor agonist. It stimulates the brain's nicotine receptors, causing the release of dopamine and reducing the symptom of nicotine withdrawal. Furthermore, varenicline blocks the receptors from nicotine-stimulated pleasure, making it less satisfying to smoke and reducing cravings. This dual mechanism of action makes varenicline a popular and effective smoking cessation medication, with clinical trial efficacy rates of approximately 45%. However, varenicline is associated with a few side effects, most commonly nausea, which can significantly impact adherence and efficacy, especially during the initiation phase of the medication.

Combination Therapies:

Studies have shown that the combination of two or three smoking cessation techniques, including medication and psychotherapy, is more effective than using only one tactic. In particular, combinations of NRT with either bupropion or varenicline have demonstrated significant efficacy in supporting smoking cessation. Combining these medications increases their individual effectiveness and reduces the intensity of withdrawal symptoms.

Behavioral Support Programs:

Behavioral support programs can be an essential component of smoking cessation therapy. These programs typically provide a range of services, such as smoking cessation counseling, a support group, and various educational materials such as quitting brochures. Programs are often offered in a group setting, wherein individuals can learn from one another's experiences. Additionally, evidence suggests that longer program duration is beneficial in increasing cessation rates. The implementation of these programs can also further enhance the effects of the smoking cessation medication by focusing on positive lifestyle changes.

Self-Help Resources:

A large number of self-help resources are available that can support individuals in their smoking cessation efforts. These resources may include online support communities, web-based interventions, self-help books, and mobile applications. While the efficacy of online and mobile resources isn't as well-established as traditional support programs, early evidence suggests that they can be helpful for the average smoker who wants to quit.

Discussion:

The use of prescription medications for smoking cessation can be effective in increasing the likelihood of successful smoking cessation in both adults and adolescents. However, their efficacy is highly dependent on several factors, including the commitment level of the individual attempting to quit, the duration of the therapy, and the dosage and type of medication used. It is necessary to identify and select the most suitable smoking cessation medication that suits the individual's particular needs to increase their odds of success. Therefore, healthcare providers must evaluate each candidate's unique preferences, medical and psychiatric history, and the severity of their nicotine addiction. Education and counseling regarding proper medication use should also be provided to support the patient's long-term success, as should setting realistic cessation goals, consistent follow-up, and ongoing support.

2. How they work and side effects

Introduction

Tobacco consumption, either in the form of smoking or snuffing, is a leading cause of preventable deaths in the world. Over the years, several nicotine replacement therapies (NRTs) have been developed to help smokers quit smoking. NRTs refer to nicotine-containing products used to wean smokers off from smoking cigarettes. They are marketed as over-the-counter (OTC) medications, and others require prescriptions. NRTs are formulated in various forms such as gums, patches, lozenges, sprays, inhalers, and nasal sprays. This article aimed to explore how NRTs work, their types, and the side effects associated with them in relation to smoking cessation.

How NRTs work

NRTs work by delivering controlled amounts of nicotine into the bloodstream. The gradual reduction in nicotine intake helps manage nicotine withdrawal symptoms, which are what causes people to relapse after quitting smoking. The intensity of the withdrawal symptoms is proportional to the depth of the dependence on nicotine and is characterized by cravings, irritability, anxiety, mood swings, difficulty concentrating, and restlessness. NRTs provide a safer means of delivering nicotine to the body since they do not expose users to harmful chemicals that come with burning tobacco, such as tar, carbon monoxide, and carcinogenic compounds.

Types of NRTs

Nicotine gums

Nicotine gum is the most popular NRT type available. It works by delivering nicotine directly into the bloodstream through the mouth tissues. The user chews the gum until nicotine is released, then places it between the cheek and gum and sucks slowly to get the nicotine absorbed by the bloodstream. Nicotine gum comes in different strengths, and users are advised to follow the manufacturer's recommended guidelines since improper use can cause negative side effects.

Nicotine patches

Nicotine patches are transdermal medications that deliver nicotine to the body through the skin. The patch is usually applied to the upper arm or a clean, dry area of the chest. The patch needs to be changed daily to maintain steady nicotine levels in the bloodstream. The efficacy of patches is highly dependent on following the manufacturer's instructions.

Nicotine inhalers

Nicotine inhalers are devices that deliver nicotine to the lungs in the form of vapor, similar to that produced by an e-cigarette. Users are cautioned not to inhale the vapor directly into the lungs but to puff it into the mouth and hold it for a while to allow nicotine absorption into the bloodstream. The inhaler usually comes with a regular puffing schedule, just like the other NRTs.

Nicotine lozenges

Nicotine lozenges are tablets containing nicotine, which are dissolved in the mouth to release nicotine. The use of lozenges involves placing them in the mouth until they are dissolved, usually between twenty minutes to an hour. Like with other NRTs, lozenges come in different strengths, and adherence to the recommended guidelines is essential.

Nicotine nasal spray

The nicotine nasal spray delivers nicotine directly to the nasal lining, where it gets transported to the bloodstream. The spray bottle comes with a nozzle that is directed towards the nose or the sinuses, and the nicotine is sprayed inside the nostrils. The nasal spray may cause nasal irritation or stinging and requires proper use.

Nicotine sublingual tablets

Nicotine sublingual tablets involve placing a tablet of nicotine under the tongue, where it dissolves and nicotine gets absorbed into the bloodstream. Sublingual tablets are convenient to use, but like other NRT forms, manufactures recommendations must be followed to avoid unpleasant side effects.

Side effects of NRTs

While NRTs are generally tolerated, there are still possible side effects that users report. The severity of the side effects is usually mild and is often a result of inadequate compliance to directions by the user. The most common side effects of NRTs include:

Nausea and vomiting

Nausea and vomiting are common side effects of NRTs, usually resulting from improper use of NRT products such as gums and lozenges. Users are advised not to chew the gum or swallow the lozenge since it reduces efficient nicotine absorption and causes these negative side effects.

Headaches

Headaches are another side effect of NRTs and are usually a result of the sudden onset of nicotine in the bloodstream. The severity of the headache varies from person to person, but it generally resolves when the intake is adjusted to the recommended dose.

Dizziness

Dizziness may occur due to low blood pressure and is common in inhalers and nasal sprays. Users are advised not to inhale the vapor directly into the lungs and to maintain the recommended puffing schedules and doses to avoid negative side effects.

Mouth ulcers

Mouth ulcers may develop due to frequent use of nicotine gum, especially if improperly chewed and swallowed. To avoid mouth ulcers, the gum must be chewed slowly with breaks in between until the nicotine taste is gone.

Insomnia

Insomnia is a possible negative side effect of NRTs and occurs due to the stimulating effect of nicotine in the body. Users are advised not to use NRT products too close to bedtime and to maintain restorative sleep environments for better sleep quality and avoiding negative side effects.

Conclusion

In conclusion, NRTs have been developed to help people quit smoking by managing withdrawal symptoms. They are available in various forms, such as gums, patches, lozenges, inhalers, nasal sprays, and sublingual tablets. Users must adhere to the recommended doses and instructions to avoid negative side effects such as nausea, headaches, dizziness, and mouth ulcers. NRTs have been known to help smokers quit smoking and improve their quality of life.

3. Using medication in combination with NRT

Introduction

Smoking is a significant public health issue worldwide. It is one of the leading causes of preventable deaths that affect millions of people every year. In developed nations, the prevalence of smoking has been steadily decreasing, but the trend is not the same in developing and underdeveloped nations. In the United States alone, smoking kills over 480,000 Americans annually, with more than 16 million living with a smoking-related disease. This is a critical issue since smoking-related diseases lead to chest pain, heart disease, stroke, lung cancer, and respiratory diseases (O'Brien, et al. 2016). To combat cigarette addiction, nicotine replacement therapy (NRT), medication, and behavioral counseling have proven effective. However, combining medication with NRT offers an even more excellent chance of quitting, with a success rate of over 30 percent. In this paper, we discuss the importance of medication in combination with NRT, factors that affect medication adherence, and potential side effects.

Medication in Combination with NRT

The use of medication and NRT has been supported by extensive research. NRTs such as patches, gum, lozenges, inhalers, and nasal sprays offer smokers a chance to transition from smoking with low levels of nicotine. Some of these methods such as patches provide a slow and steady release of nicotine into the bloodstream. Smokers, in essence, continue to get their nicotine supply without exposure to other harmful substances in cigarette smoke. According to O'Brien, et al. (2016), nicotine replacement therapy alone increases the likelihood of smoking cessation by one-and-a-half to twofold.

However, medication in combination with NRT boosts the chance of quitting even further. Medications such as Varenicline (Chantix), Bupropion (Zyban), and Clonidine improve the chances of quitting by more than 30%. In one trial, Varenicline and NRT aids resulted in a smoking cessation rate of 50% (Jorenby, et al., 2006). Therefore, combining medication with NRT can significantly increase an individual's chances of quitting smoking for good.

Factors Affecting Medication Adherence

Medication adherence refers to the extent to which a patient takes medication as prescribed by their doctor. According to the World Health Organization (WHO), medication adherence is a complex behavior influenced by several factors, including socioeconomic, healthcare system-related, patient-related, and therapy-related factors (WHO, 2003). In the case of using medication in combination with NRT, factors such as the complexity of the regimen, side effects, personal responsibility, and educational levels may affect medication adherence.

The complexity of the regimen refers to the number of pills taken daily, timing, and administration. Adherence is likely to decrease if the medication regimen is complex, leading to missed doses that may impact effectiveness. In addition, the side effects of medication and NRTs, such as nausea, vomiting, and dizziness, may discourage adherence, affecting cessation rates (Stead, et al. 2013). Personal responsibility and discipline are also crucial in the adherence to medication. Patients may not stick to their medication regimen if they do not believe in the effectiveness of the medication or fail to adhere to periodic follow-up doctor visits. Finally, the level of education may impact medication adherence, especially in patients who do not speak the language in which the prescription is written.

Potential Side Effects

Varenicline, Bupropion, and Clonidine are some of the medication prescribed alongside NRT to aid in smoking cessation. However, like all medications, they have potential side effects. The most common side effects of Bupropion include dry mouth, palpitations, nausea, and insomnia, while those of Clonidine include drowsiness, dry mouth, dizziness, and constipation (FAA. 2018). Varenicline, on the other hand, may cause nausea, insomnia, and headaches (Chapman et al., 2014). In rare instances, Varenicline has been associated with psychiatric complications, such as suicidal thoughts and depression.

While the side effects can be disruptive, they are often outweighed by the benefits. Mild side effects may diminish over time, but patients should seek medical advice if the side-effects persist. Therefore, it is essential to be aware of the possible side effects of each medication and report any concerns to your doctor.

Adapting Medication Regimens to Suit Patient Needs

The effectiveness of medication in smoking cessation is often influenced by the adaptability of medication regimens. For example, Bupropion is often prescribed as a sustained-release formulation, meaning that it is released into the bloodstream over a certain period. In some cases, patients may need immediate relief from a craving or desire to smoke, and the sustained-release Bupropion formulation may not be suitable. In this case, Bupropion or Varenicline immediate-release formulations may be prescribed to suit the patient's needs (Cahill, Lindson-Hawley & Hartmann-Boyce, 2016).

Similarly, certain medications may not be suitable for individuals with pre-existing conditions or those on medication. For example, patients with hypertension may not be cefontrona (Clonidine) due to its blood pressure-lowering effects. Varenicline may also have interactions with certain medications, such as insulin, which should be monitored by the physician. Therefore, the medication regimen should be adapted to suit the patient's individual needs, with constant monitoring by a physician.

Conclusion

Smoking remains a significant public health issue worldwide, with millions of people dying annually from smoking-related diseases. The use of nicotine replacement therapy (NRT), medication, and behavioral counseling are effective in smoking cessation. However, combining medication with NRT increases the chance of quitting smoking by over 30%. Medication in combination with NRT can be challenging, affecting factors such as medication adherence. The complexity of the regimen, side effects, personal responsibility, and educational levels may affect medication adherence. Finally, the possible side effects, although rare, can be treated by constant monitoring by physicians and adapting the medication regimen to suit the patient's needs. In conclusion, using medication in combination with NRT can significantly increase the chances of quitting smoking for good.

References

Cahill, K., Lindson-Hawley, N. & Hartmann-Boyce, J. (2016) Nicotine-replacement therapy for smoking cessation. The New England Journal of Medicine. 375(26), pp. 2550-2552.

Chapman, S. & Freeman, B. (2014). Markers of the denormalization of smoking and the tobacco industry. Tobacco Control. 23(Suppl 1), pp. i23-i30.

Federal Aviation Administration (FAA) (2018), Bupropion. Retrieved on 05 May 2021 from https://www.faa.gov/about/office_org/ headquarters_offices/avs/offices/aam/drug_alcohol/content/ deidentified/faa_approved_drugs/bupropion_deidentified.pdf

Jorenby, D. E., Hays, J. T., Rigotti, N. A., Azoulay, S., Watsky, E. J., Williams, K. E., ... Hurt, R. D. (2006). Efficacy of varenicline, an alpha4beta2 nicotinic acetylcholine receptor partial agonist, vs placebo or sustained-release bupropion for smoking cessation: a randomized controlled trial. JAMA, 296(1), 56–63.

O'Brien, B. & Balfour, D. (2016) Smoking and nicotine addiction: A review of treatments and methods. Journal of Addiction Research and Therapy. 7(2), pp. 1000173.

Stead, L. E., Perera, R., Bullen, C., Mant, D., Lancaster, T. (2013) Nicotine replacement therapy for smoking cessation. The Cochrane Database of Systematic Reviews (5). CD000146.

World Health Organization (WHO). Adherence to long-term therapies: Evidence for action. Switzerland: World Health Organization; 2003.

4. Quiz

1. What prescription medication can be used as a nicotine replacement therapy?
    A. Bupropion
    B. Varenicline
    C. Nicotine gum
    D. Clonidine

Answer: B. Varenicline

2. What over-the-counter medication can be used as a nicotine replacement therapy?
    A. Bupropion
    B. Varenicline
    C. Nicotine gum
    D. Clonidine

Answer: C. Nicotine gum

3. What prescription medication works by reducing cravings and withdrawal symptoms?
    A. Bupropion
    B. Varenicline
    C. Nicotine gum
    D. Clonidine

Answer: A. Bupropion

4. What prescription medication can be used to help manage nicotine withdrawal symptoms in smokers?
    A. Bupropion
    B. Varenicline
    C. Nicotine gum
    D. Clonidine

Answer: D. Clonidine

5. What type of medication should be avoided by smokers who are also using nicotine replacement therapy?
    A. Antidepressants
    B. Blood thinners
    C. Pain medications
    D. Stimulants

Answer: D. Stimulants

VI. Behavioral Therapy

1. Different types of behavioral therapy

Introduction:

Smoking has been a major health concern globally, contributing to over 7 million deaths annually according to the World Health Organization (WHO). The habit is estimated to cause approximately 1 in every 5 deaths in the United States every year. Cigarette smoking leads to an array of health problems including respiratory diseases, heart disease, stroke, and cancer. However, despite the potential health risks associated with smoking, most smokers find it challenging to quit. This is primarily due to the addiction and withdrawal symptoms that often accompany quitting smoking. Thankfully, there are numerous behavioral therapies that can help individuals stop smoking. Behavioral therapy involves modifying behavior and changing an individual's cognitive processes to bring about positive change. This paper will explore several types of behavioral therapies that can be used to help individuals stop smoking.

Cognitive Behavior Therapy (CBT)

Cognitive Behavior Therapy is a type of psychotherapy that is focused on modifying behavior by changing how individuals think and feel in response to internal and external stimuli, particularly negative thoughts and emotions. CBT for smoking cessation involves identifying and challenging negative thoughts and beliefs that may hamper an individual's efforts to quit smoking. This therapy is based on the premise that negative thoughts and emotions are the primary drivers of cigarette smoking and that these can be changed by altering one's belief system.

One of the most common approaches used in CBT for smoking cessation is the technique of cognitive restructuring. This technique involves identifying negative and irrational thoughts, evaluating them objectively, and replacing them with more rational thoughts and beliefs. For example, a smoker may have the belief that smoking is part of their identity, and giving up smoking will mean losing part of their identity. The therapist may challenge this belief by asking the smoker to identify other things that make up their identity, such as their relationships, hobbies, or work. By doing this, the smoker is encouraged to think more positively about themselves and their life, rather than relying on smoking to form part of their identity.

Another popular approach used in CBT for smoking cessation is Exposure Therapy. This technique involves exposing the smoker to triggers that induce the craving for cigarettes, such as pictures of cigarettes, smokers, or smoking areas. By confronting and overcoming these triggers, individuals learn to tolerate and control their urge to smoke, thereby helping them to quit smoking more effectively.

Contingency Management (CM)

Contingency Management (CM) is a behavioral therapy that seeks to reinforce positive behavior through rewards. The goal of CM is to reinforce the cessation of smoking and discourage the individual from relapsing into the habit. This is achieved through providing incentives to the individual upon successfully quitting smoking or abstaining from smoking for a designated period. The rewards typically involve tangible items such as vouchers, cash, or prizes.

To be effective, CM requires specific, measurable, achievable, realistic, and time-bound (SMART) goals. The therapist and the smoker work together to develop a plan of action that outlines the desired behavior and the rewards to be offered upon successful cessation or abstinence from smoking. For instance, if the individual refrains from smoking for a week, they may receive $20, and if they abstain for a month, they may receive a more significant reward. The goal is to ensure that the rewards serve as a motivation to quit smoking and help to overcome the addiction and withdrawal symptoms.

Behavioral Therapy and Pharmacotherapy

Behavioral Therapy and Pharmacotherapy are often combined in smoking cessation programs to increase the likelihood of success. The pharmacotherapeutic component is used to address the physical addiction to nicotine, while behavioral therapy helps to address the psychological dependence on smoking. Research suggests that the combination of these two therapies results in a higher success rate in quitting smoking than either therapy alone.

Nicotine Replacement Therapy (NRT) is a common pharmacotherapeutic approach used in smoking cessation programs. NRT involves the use of products such as nicotine gum, patches, lozenges, or inhalers to provide smokers with a controlled and measured dose of nicotine, which helps to reduce the symptoms of withdrawal. In conjunction with behavioral therapy, NRT can help to reduce the likelihood of relapse and to increase the probability of long-term success in quitting smoking.

Motivational Interviewing (MI)

Motivational Interviewing (MI) is a person-centered approach to behavior change frequently used in smoking cessation programs. MI is a collaborative approach that is focused on exploring and resolving ambivalence towards quitting smoking. Ambivalence refers to holding mixed feelings or contradictory ideas. For instance, a smoker may want to quit smoking but may feel anxious or apprehensive about the quitting process.

The goal of MI is to increase the smoker's motivation to quit smoking by exploring and resolving ambivalence. The approach seeks to create a safe, empathetic, and non-judgmental environment where the smoker can feel comfortable discussing their concerns and fears about quitting smoking. The therapist collaborates with the smoker in exploring their reasons to quit smoking and helps to identify and overcome the barriers that may be hindering their efforts. This approach is effective in helping individuals to overcome the addictive nature of smoking and to develop the confidence needed to quit smoking.

Mindfulness-Based Cognitive Therapy (MBCT)

Mindfulness-Based Cognitive Therapy (MBCT) is a type of behavioral therapy that combines the principles of mindfulness with cognitive therapy techniques. MBCT involves training the smoker to develop a non-judgmental awareness of their thoughts and feelings regarding smoking. The approach seeks to help smokers better understand their smoking triggers and to develop skills to manage their urges.

The practice of mindfulness involves being present in the moment, non-judgmentally observing one's thoughts and emotions. Mindfulness meditation can help smokers to detach from their smoking triggers and to recognize that cravings are temporary and will pass. This detachment can help smokers to overcome the urge to smoke and to develop a new perspective on smoking.

Conclusion:

Behavioral therapies are effective strategies for addressing smoking cessation. These therapies focus on modifying behavior, changing an individual's cognitive processes, and reinforcing positive behavior through rewards. The approaches explored in this paper include Cognitive Behavioral Therapy (CBT), Contingency Management (CM), Behavioral Therapy and Pharmacotherapy, Motivational Interviewing (MI), and Mindfulness-Based Cognitive Therapy (MBCT). While each approach is unique, all are effective strategies for helping individuals overcome the challenges associated with quitting smoking. The choice of therapy will depend on the individual's unique circumstances and preferences. However, what is most important is for individuals to seek help to quit smoking and to work with a qualified therapist or counselor to ensure long-term success.

2. Counseling options and support groups

Introduction

Cigarette smoking has always been one of the biggest public health issues in the world today. It is estimated that smoking-related illnesses kill more than half a million people every year in the United States alone. In addition, cigarette smoking is a major cause of heart diseases, lung cancer, and many other health problems. Despite of all these statistics, millions of people around the world continue to smoke. So, in this paper, I will discuss various counseling options and support groups that can help smokers quit smoking.

Counseling Options

There are many counseling options available for smokers who want to quit smoking. These options include individual counseling, group counseling, telephone counseling, and online counseling.

Individual Counseling

Individual counseling is a one-on-one session between a smoker and a trained counselor. During these sessions, the smoker can discuss the various reasons that led to their smoking habit and how they can overcome the addiction. The counselor will also provide the smoker with information on the dangers of smoking and the benefits of quitting. This kind of counseling is ideal for people who are shy or introverted and find it hard to express their feelings and thoughts in public or in a group setting.

Group Counseling

Group counseling is another option for smokers who want to quit smoking. This type of counseling involves a group of people who come together to support and encourage each other to quit smoking. Group counseling sessions are usually led by a professionally trained counselor who guides discussions and offers advice. This kind of counseling is ideal for people who feel more comfortable sharing their feelings and thoughts in a group setting.

Telephone Counseling

Telephone counseling is a convenient counseling option for individuals who cannot attend in-person counseling sessions. This kind of counseling usually involves a trained counselor providing support and advice over the phone. The counselor may also offer additional support through emails or text messages.

Online Counseling

Another counseling option is online counseling. This type of counseling usually involves a trained counselor providing support and advice through emails, text messaging, or video conferencing. Online counseling is ideal for people who have busy schedules or live in remote areas where in-person counseling may not be available. However, it should be noted that online counseling may not be suitable for everyone, especially those who do not have access to the internet or those who prefer face-to-face counseling.

Support Groups

Support groups are another effective way to help smokers quit smoking. These groups provide a safe and supportive environment where smokers can come together to share their experiences, struggles, and successes in quitting smoking.

Nicotine Anonymous

Nicotine Anonymous is a support group designed for smokers who want to quit smoking. Nicotine Anonymous meetings usually involve a group of people who share their experiences and offer support to those trying to quit smoking. The meetings usually follow a 12-step program similar to Alcoholics Anonymous. Nicotine Anonymous meetings provide smokers with a supportive community and a sense of accountability.

Quit Smoking Online Forum

Quit Smoking Online Forum is an online community where smokers can connect with other people who are also trying to quit smoking. The forum provides a platform for smokers to share experiences, offer support, and ask questions. The online forum is available 24 hours a day, seven days a week, making it easy for smokers to access support whenever they need it.

American Lung Association's Freedom from Smoking Online Program

The American Lung Association's Freedom from Smoking Online Program is an online program designed to help smokers quit smoking. The program offers a self-paced course that takes smokers through all the steps in quitting smoking. The program also includes discussion boards where smokers can connect with each other and share experiences. The program provides smokers with information, tools, and support they need to quit smoking successfully.

Conclusion

In conclusion, smoking is a dangerous habit that can cause a wide range of health problems. Fortunately, there are many counseling options and support groups available for smokers who want to quit smoking. Counseling options such as individual counseling, group counseling, telephone counseling, and online counseling offer smokers the opportunity to talk to professionals and get advice on how to quit smoking. Meanwhile, support groups such as Nicotine Anonymous, Quit Smoking Online Forum, and American Lung Association's Freedom from Smoking Online Program provide smokers with a supportive community where they can share experiences and get support from others who are also trying to quit smoking. By taking advantage of these counseling options and support groups, smokers can find the right support and encouragement to help them quit smoking for good.

3. Strategies for dealing with cravings and triggers

Introduction

Smoking is a common and serious habit that has vast negative effects on individuals' health and wellbeing. Despite the significant efforts and awareness creation about the negative impacts of smoking, it remains challenging for individuals to cease smoking. This is because smokers develop cravings and triggers that make it difficult to stop smoking. Smokers' cravings and triggers are largely driven by psychological and physical factors such as an attachment to nicotine and mental stress. Therefore, developing strategies for dealing with cravings and triggers is essential to overcome smoking addiction. This article will discuss various strategies for dealing with cravings and triggers on how to stop smoking.

What are Cravings and Triggers?

Cravings refer to the intense urge to engage in an addictive behavior, such as smoking. Cravings are usually driven by psychological factors such as stress, depression, anxiety, or a sense of reward. They typically aim to reduce individuals' negative emotions and increase positive feelings. Triggers correspond to situations, people, and environments that stimulate smokers to start smoking again. These triggers can range from people, situations, or objects like cigarettes, lighters, ashtrays, stress, or a certain environment. Smokers often experience cravings and triggers simultaneously, which makes it hard to break their smoking habit. Therefore, it's essential to develop strategies to manage cravings and triggers.

Strategies for Dealing with Cravings and Triggers

1. Mindfulness

Mindfulness refers to the ability to focus one's attention on the present moment. It helps individuals become self-aware and control their thoughts and emotions when triggered to smoke. Mindfulness encourages individuals to observe their thoughts, emotions, and physical sensations non-judgmentally. This means being aware of cravings and triggers without trying to control them or giving in to them. Mindfulness teaches individuals not to judge themselves harshly and develop self-compassion. Mindfulness-based interventions such as mindful breathing, meditation, and yoga can reduce cravings, anxiety, and stress in smokers.

2. Nicotine Replacement Therapy

Nicotine replacement therapy (NRT) involves using pharmacological products that provide nicotine to the body, such as nicotine gum, lozenges, patches, and inhalers. NRT helps relieve smokers' physical symptoms of nicotine withdrawal, keep withdrawal symptoms at bay, and reduce cravings to smoke. The use of NRT can lead to less irritability and stress, as well as reduce the probability of returning to smoking when faced with triggers. However, despite its benefits, NRT alone is not enough to overcome smoking addiction. It is essential to combine NRT with other smoking cessation strategies.

3. Distracti on and Avoidance

Distracting oneself from smoking triggers and cravings can be a useful strategy when trying to quit smoking. This can include taking a walk, engaging in a new hobby, or interacting with friends and family. Distraction keeps the mind off cravings and reduces the likeliness of succumbing to smoking triggers. Additionally, avoidance strategy involves staying away from situations and people that can stimulate smoking behaviors. Avoiding the environments and people that one used to smoke with can help break the association of smoking with particular experiences or circumstances, making it easier to overcome smoking.

4. Exercise

Exercise is a useful strategy for handling smoking cravings and triggers. Exercise helps to release endorphins, chemicals in the brain that promote a positive feeling, mental clarity, and reduced stress. This helps minimize the likelihood of reverting to smoking behavior when experiencing cravings and triggers. Engaging in regular exercise reduces anxiety, depression, and stress, factors that are likely to cause cravings.

5. Seeking Professional Help

Seeking professional help is an effective approach to help individuals overcome smoking addiction. Professional help provides individuals with information, guidance, and support to help them quit smoking. This can include joining support groups, counseling by trained professionals, or using pharmacological interventions such as antidepressants. Professional interventions can help smokers identify and overcome the psychological, physical, and social factors that contribute to smoking behaviors. Professional interventions offer coping mechanisms that can be useful during smoking triggers and cravings.

6. Changing Beliefs and Attitudes

Beliefs and attitudes play a significant role in smoking behavior. Individuals who hold negative beliefs and attitudes toward smoking are more likely to develop smoking addiction. Individuals need to change their beliefs and attitudes towards smoking to overcome the addiction. By understanding the health implications of smoking and developing a positive self-concept, individuals can have the motivation to quit smoking. A positive self-concept is essential as it helps one's self-esteem, self-efficacy, and confidence to make changes in their behavior to cease smoking addiction.

Conclusion

In conclusion, smoking is an addictive behavior that is challenging to overcome. The cravings and triggers that smokers experience when trying to quit smoking can be significant barriers to quitting smoking. Strategies for dealing with cravings and triggers are, therefore, essential to overcome smoking addiction. Such strategies include mindfulness, nicotine replacement therapy, distraction and avoidance, exercise, seeking professional help, and changing beliefs and attitudes. Implementing these strategies can help reduce cravings, manage triggers, and build resilience to overcome smoking addiction. Therefore, it's essential to select a strategy that suits one's personality, needs, and characteristics. It's also essential to have patience, perseverance, and support from loved ones when undergoing the process of quitting smoking.

4. Quiz

1. What is the key principle behind behavioral therapy for quitting smoking?
    A) Decreasing nicotine consumption gradually
    B) Addressing underlying emotional issues
    C) Changing harmful behavioral patterns
    D) None of the above

Answer: C) Changing harmful behavioral patterns

2. Which of the following is NOT an example of a smoking cessation strategy that utilizes behavioral therapy?
    A) Rewarding yourself for reaching quitting milestones
    B) Avoiding smoking triggers
    C) Using nicotine gum or patches
    D) Setting a quit date

Answer: C) Using nicotine gum or patches (this is not a strategy exclusive to behavioral therapy)

3. What is a commonly used technique in behavioral therapy called that involves tracking smoking behavior and patterns?
    A) Cognitive restructuring
    B) Mindfulness meditation
    C) Contingency management
    D) Self-monitoring

Answer: D) Self-monitoring

4. What is a key component of contingency management in smoking cessation?
    A) Replacing smoking with a new habit
    B) Using positive reinforcement to encourage quitting behavior
    C) Identifying negative consequences of smoking
    D) None of the above

Answer: B) Using positive reinforcement to encourage quitting behavior

5. What is one way to address negative thoughts and beliefs that may hinder quitting smoking?
    A) Avoiding triggers for negative thinking
    B) Challenging your negative thoughts and replacing them with more positive ones
    C) Using nicotine replacement therapy
    D) None of the above

Answer: B) Challenging your negative thoughts and replacing them with more positive ones

VII. Staying Smoke-Free

1. Coping with withdrawal symptoms

Introduction

Smoking is one of the leading causes of preventable deaths worldwide. Smoking cessation is one of the best ways to reduce the risk of developing tobacco-related diseases. However, quitting smoking is not an easy process. It requires a lot of will power, determination, and commitment. Nicotine is a highly addictive substance, and its withdrawal symptoms can be very challenging to deal with. Coping with withdrawal symptoms is one of the most crucial aspects of quitting smoking. This paper will explore coping strategies that can be used to manage withdrawal symptoms in relation to how to stop smoking.

Understanding withdrawal symptoms

Quitting smoking causes a lot of physical and psychological changes in the body. Nicotine withdrawal symptoms can begin as soon as two hours after the last cigarette and can peak within the first few days. Withdrawal symptoms vary from person to person, but they include physical, mental, and emotional symptoms such as:

Physical symptoms
- Headaches
- Coughing
- Fatigue

- Sweating
- Shaking
- Nausea and vomiting

Mental symptoms
- Irritability
- Anxiety
- Restlessness
- Difficulty concentrating
- Insomnia

Emotional symptoms
- Depression
- Mood swings
- Cravings
- Loss of appetite
- Weight gain

While the severity and duration of withdrawal symptoms vary, they can be particularly challenging for individuals trying to quit smoking. However, understanding the symptoms and having a plan in place to cope with them is critical to achieving successful smoking cessation.

Coping with withdrawal symptoms

1. Nicotine replacement therapy

One of the most popular methods for dealing with nicotine withdrawal symptoms is nicotine replacement therapy (NRT). NRT is a treatment that provides smokers with a lower dose of nicotine in other forms such as chewing gum, patches, lozenges, or nasal sprays to reduce the impact of nicotine withdrawal symptoms. For example, nicotine gum works by releasing small amounts of nicotine into the body to help alleviate cravings, and the patch supplies a steady and low dose of nicotine to ease withdrawal symptoms gradually. It is essential to seek the advice of a healthcare professional on which NRT treatment is most suitable for your specific needs.

2. Medications

Several medications, such as Bupropion and Varenicline, can help smokers quit by reducing cravings and withdrawal symptoms. Bupropion works by interfering with the reuptake of dopamine, norepinephrine and Varenicline works by reducing the rewarding effects of nicotine on the brain. These medications can only be obtained through a doctor's prescription and require careful management and monitoring by the physician.

3. Exercise and relaxation techniques

Exercise helps to reduce stress and anxiety, which are common nicotine withdrawal symptoms. Exercising increases endorphins, which boosts mood and promotes a sense of well-being. Additionally, relaxation techniques such as yoga, deep breathing, and meditation are also helpful in reducing withdrawal symptoms, as they promote relaxation and reduce anxiety.

4. Healthy diet and hydration

Quitting smoking can affect an individual's appetite and dietary habits. It is important to consume a balanced diet that is rich in nutrients, such as protein, fruits, and vegetables. A healthy diet can help maintain energy levels, boost the immune system, and promote a healthier body weight. Staying hydrated by drinking water and avoiding caffeine and alcohol can also be helpful in reducing nicotine cravings and alleviating withdrawal symptoms.

5. Support groups and counseling

Quitting smoking can be an isolating experience. Support groups and counseling can provide a supportive environment that helps individuals stay motivated and focused on their smoking cessation goals. There are many groups and organizations that provide free counseling services, which can help smokers deal with withdrawal symptoms and cravings. The support of family, friends, or healthcare professionals can also make a significant impact on the success of quitting smoking.

6. Mindfulness and distraction techniques

Mindfulness is a technique that allows individuals to focus on the present moment and to observe their thoughts and feelings without judgment. Mindfulness can help individuals deal with the anxiety and stress that comes with nicotine withdrawal symptoms. Distraction techniques, such as engaging in a new hobby or spending time with friends and family, are also helpful in reducing cravings and smoking-related thoughts.

Conclusion

Quitting smoking is a challenging process that requires a lot of commitment and perseverance. Coping with nicotine withdrawal symptoms is an essential part of this process. Withdrawal symptoms can be challenging to deal with, and it is vital to seek support and use coping strategies to ease the physical and emotional impact of quitting smoking. Understanding the withdrawal symptoms and having an action plan in place for coping with them is critical to the success of smoking cessation. It is essential to know that quitting smoking is a journey and that with the right mindset, support, and motivation, it can be achieved.

2. Preventing relapse

Introduction

Smoking has been identified as one of the leading causes of preventable deaths worldwide, and it poses a significant threat to public health (World Health Organization, 2021). While most smokers are aware of the adverse health effects associated with smoking, they continue to smoke, and the cessation process seems to be challenging and often characterized by relapse. Relapse refers to the recurrence of smoking behavior after a period of abstinence. The main reason why smokers find the cessation process challenging is that nicotine is a highly addictive substance, and withdrawal symptoms can be severe, both physically and mentally. Relapse rates are high among individuals who attempt to quit smoking, and it has been estimated that over 90% of those who quit will relapse within one year (Hughes, 2020). Therefore, preventing relapse remains a critical factor in achieving long-term smoking cessation. This paper aims to provide an overview of ways to prevent relapse in relation to how to stop smoking.

The Role of Nicotine Addiction in Relapse

Nicotine addiction is one of the main reasons why smokers find it challenging to quit smoking. Nicotine is a highly addictive substance that affects the brain's reward system, leading to the release of dopamine, a neurotransmitter that creates a feeling of pleasure and satisfaction (Benowitz, 2010). Smokers who are unsuccessful in their cessation attempts often relapse because nicotine withdrawal symptoms, such as anxiety, depression, irritability, and cravings, can be overwhelming. It is estimated that nicotine withdrawal symptoms peak within two to three days after quitting and can last for several weeks (Hughes, 2020). Consequently, the intense cravings and withdrawal symptoms often lead to relapse, and smokers find themselves back to their old habit.

Therefore, preventing relapse in relation to quitting smoking involves reducing the nicotine dependence that leads to intense cravings and withdrawal symptoms. One way of achieving this is by using nicotine replacement therapy (NRT), which delivers nicotine to the body without the harmful effects of smoking. NRT is available in various forms, including patches, gum, lozenges, inhalers, and nasal spray. The primary benefit of NRT is that it reduces the intensity of nicotine cravings and withdrawal symptoms, making it easier for smokers to quit and remain abstinent. However, it is essential to use NRT under the guidance of a healthcare professional because using too much or too little nicotine can be counterproductive and may lead to relapse.

Developing Coping Mechanisms

Another critical factor in preventing relapse while quitting smoking is developing effective coping mechanisms to manage the stressors that often trigger smoking behavior. Stress and anxiety are significant predictors of smoking behavior, and smokers often use cigarettes to manage their emotions or cope with stressful situations. Therefore, developing alternative coping mechanisms is crucial to preventing relapse. Coping mechanisms can include relaxation techniques such as deep breathing, meditation, or yoga. Exercise has also been shown to reduce stress and improve mental health, making it an effective coping mechanism that can help prevent relapse.

Another useful coping mechanism is cognitive-behavioral therapy (CBT), a type of psychotherapy that focuses on modifying maladaptive thoughts and behaviors that lead to relapse. CBT is an evidence-based treatment for quitting smoking that teaches individuals how to identify and challenge negative thought patterns that lead to smoking behavior. CBT also provides individuals with skills to manage the triggers that lead to smoking behavior, such as stress, social situations, and cravings.

Support and Accountability

Support and accountability are other critical factors in preventing relapse while quitting smoking. Quitting smoking can be a challenging process, and having a support system in place can make a significant difference in achieving long-term abstinence. Support can come from a healthcare professional, a support group, family, or friends who provide encouragement, motivation, and accountability throughout the quitting process. Support can also come in the form of online forums or chat rooms where individuals can share their experiences, ask questions, and provide support to each other.

Accountability is another effective way to prevent relapse while quitting smoking. This can come in different forms, such as setting a quit date and sharing it with a friend or family member, working with a healthcare professional to develop a quit plan, or using a quit smoking app that tracks progress and provides reminders. Accountability helps individuals stay committed to their quitting goals and motivates them to overcome challenges and barriers that may arise during the process.

Avoiding Triggers

Avoiding triggers that may lead to smoking behavior is another critical factor in preventing relapse. Triggers are events, situations, or emotions that lead to smoking behavior. Triggers can include social situations, stress, or negative emotions such as sadness, anxiety, or boredom. Therefore, identifying and avoiding triggers is crucial to preventing relapse. One way to avoid triggers is by creating a smoke-free environment, removing any smoking paraphernalia such as ashtrays, lighters, or cigarettes. This can reduce the likelihood of smoking behavior and help an individual remain abstinent.

Another useful strategy is to replace smoking behavior with a healthier activity or habit, such as going for a walk, reading a book, or listening to music. These healthy habits can help distract individuals from the cravings or urges to smoke and provide a healthier way to manage stress and other triggers that may lead to smoking behavior.

Conclusion

In conclusion, preventing relapse is a critical factor in achieving long-term smoking cessation. Nicotine addiction is one of the main reasons why smokers find it challenging to quit smoking, and withdrawal symptoms such as intense cravings and anxiety often lead to relapse. Therefore, reducing nicotine dependence through NRT, developing effective coping mechanisms such as CBT, having support and accountability, and avoiding triggers that may lead to smoking behavior are key strategies in preventing relapse. Quitting smoking can be a challenging process, and individuals may experience several relapses before achieving long-term abstinence. However, with the right strategies, tools, and support, individuals can overcome the challenges and achieve their quitting goals.

3. Managing stress and staying motivated

Introduction

Smoking is a dangerous and addictive habit that can lead to serious health issues, including heart disease, lung cancer, and other respiratory diseases. However, quitting smoking is not an easy task, as many tobacco users suffer from anxiety, stress, and other psychological issues when they try to quit. Managing stress and staying motivated are crucial aspects when it comes to quitting smoking.

Stress and Smoking

Stress is one of the main reasons why many people start smoking, and it is also one of the biggest obstacles to quitting smoking. Nicotine is a stimulant, and therefore, smokers tend to feel relaxed and more focused when smoking. However, the relaxation and calming effect of smoking are temporary and cause more stress and anxiety in the long run. The psychological dependence on nicotine is so strong that it can quickly become the go-to coping mechanism for stress, even when it becomes a health hazard.

According to research, the majority of smokers who try to quit smoking will relapse within the first few weeks because of stress and anxiety. Therefore, it is important to find ways to manage stress in order to quit smoking successfully.

Managing Stress

There are several strategies that smokers can use for managing stress, including:

1. Exercise - Exercise is one of the most effective ways to relieve stress. When you exercise, your body releases endorphins, which are natural mood boosters that can help reduce stress levels. A daily exercise routine can also divert attention away from smoking, and improve physical and mental health.

2. Mindfulness Meditation - Mindfulness meditation involves focusing the mind on the present moment and acknowledging one's thoughts, feelings, and surroundings without judgment. It has been shown to reduce stress and anxiety and helps one become more resilient in dealing with stress.

3. Deep Breathing - Deep breathing is a simple and quick stress management technique. It involves taking slow and deep breaths, holding for a few seconds and then exhaling slowly. By focusing on your breath, you can activate the body's natural relaxation response.

4. Listening to Music - Listening to relaxing music is another effective way to reduce stress. Music has the ability to lower the heart rate, lower blood pressure and helps distract the mind from negative thoughts.

5. Social Support - Social support is important for stress management. Having people to talk to about one's feelings and challenges can help reduce stress levels and provide a sense of comfort and motivation.

6. Mindful Eating - Being mindful when eating can be helpful when managing stress. Paying attention to the taste and texture of food helps in relaxation and kindness towards oneself.

Staying Motivated

Staying motivated when quitting smoking is important because it helps smokers stay on track and overcome the various hurdles that come with cessation.

1. Setting Goals - Setting goals is a way to keep oneself motivated. Goals should be specific, measurable, achievable, relevant and time-bound (SMART). When choosing a goal, it's important to identify why one wants to quit, and keep track of progress to remain motivated.

2. Keeping a Journal - Keeping a journal is a good way to track progress and reflect on how quitting smoking is impacting one's life. Writing down reasons for quitting, struggles, and successes can help keep one focused and stay motivated.

3. Rewarding oneself - Rewarding oneself for milestones achieved is a great way to stay motivated. Rewards can be anything from going out to dinner to buying oneself something to celebrate success.

4. Joining a Support Group - A support group provides a sense of community and accountability. Communicating with those who have shared challenges and experiences, sharing tips and encouragement keeps one motivated.

5. Visualizing Success - Visualizing success and the benefits of a smoke-free life is a powerful tool for staying motivated. Visualizing oneself being healthy, energized, and happy helps overcome the challenges of quitting smoking.

Conclusion

Quitting smoking is a demanding and challenging process that requires patience, resilience, and a strong will. Stress and lack of motivation are two major barriers to success, and therefore, smokers must learn to manage their stress and stay motivated throughout the process. Incorporating stress management techniques and motivational strategies into their plans can help smokers overcome hurdles and improve their chances of quitting smoking successfully. With the right mindset, support, and strategy, anyone can quit smoking and live a healthier and happier life.

4. Celebrating milestones and accomplishments

Introduction

Smoking is a habit that has been in existence for centuries and has claimed millions of lives across the globe. Despite mounting evidence on the dangers of smoking, billions of people across the world still indulge in it. According to the World Health Organization (WHO), smoking kills approximately eight million people every year. This translates to one person dying every six seconds due to smoking-related illnesses. The good news is that with the help of professionals, determination, and the right support methods, people can quit smoking and lead healthy and fulfilling lives. Celebrating milestones and accomplishments is one of the aspects that play a crucial role in quitting smoking. This essay explores how to stop smoking and achieving milestones as a crucial aspect of enhancing the chances of quitting smoking.

Health benefits of quitting smoking

Quitting smoking is beneficial to health as it reduces the risk of developing life-threatening diseases. Smoking is the leading preventable cause of death globally, and quitting smoking is the best way to avoid the related diseases. According to the American Cancer Society, quitting smoking improves lung function and reduces the risk of lung cancer. Additionally, it reduces the risk of developing chronic obstructive pulmonary disease (COPD) and heart disease. Quitting smoking also reduces the effects of secondhand smoke on those around a smoker, as it exposes them to the same diseases that smokers are vulnerable to.

Approaches to quitting smoking

There are a variety of approaches that people can use to quit smoking, and the choice largely depends on the individual. Some of the common approaches that people use to quit smoking include:

1. Cold turkey – This approach involves stopping smoking without any external help. It requires a lot of discipline and determination as it is associated with withdrawal symptoms such as irritability, anxiety, and depression.

2. Nicotine replacement therapy – Nicotine replacement therapy (NRT) is the use of products such as nicotine patches, gum, and lozenges to help quit smoking. NRT works by providing the body with a low level of nicotine that helps reduce withdrawal symptoms.

3. Prescription medications – Several prescription medications, including varenicline and bupropion, can help quit smoking by reducing cravings and withdrawal symptoms.

4. Behavioral therapy – This approach involves seeking professional help from a therapist who helps to change behaviors associated with smoking.

5. Support groups – Joining a support group provides individuals with a platform to share their experiences with others who are also quitting smoking.

Celebrating milestones in quitting smoking

Quitting smoking is not an easy process, and requires a lot of determination and willpower. Celebrating milestones and accomplishments is an excellent way of keeping motivated during the quit journey. Celebrating milestones can be done in various ways, depending on the individual. Some of the ways to celebrate important milestones in quitting smoking include:

1. Create a quit plan – Before quitting smoking, it is essential to set realistic goals and identify ways of achieving them. Celebrating milestones helps to review progress and stay on track.

2. Create a reward system – Setting up a reward system is one of the best ways of celebrating milestones in the journey to quit smoking. Rewards can be as simple as taking a walk in the park, treating oneself to a favorite meal or drink, or buying a new outfit.

3. Share success stories – Sharing success stories with others who are also quitting smoking creates a sense of community and motivation. Joining a support group helps to connect people with similar experiences, and sharing success stories during meetings helps to keep everyone motivated.

4. Set up a savings account – Smoking is a costly habit, and quitting smoking is a great way to save money. Setting up a savings account helps to track how much one has saved because of quitting smoking, and the savings can be used for other purposes such as travel or investing.

5. Keep a journal – Keeping a journal helps to document the progress made during the journey to quit smoking. Recording the struggles and successes helps to identify areas that need improvement and celebrate accomplishments.

Benefits of celebrating accomplishments in quitting smoking

Celebrating accomplishments in quitting smoking has many benefits, including:

1. Enhanced motivation – Celebrating milestones provides a sense of accomplishment that motivates an individual to continue in the journey to quit smoking.

2. Improved self-esteem – Celebrating accomplishments provides a sense of pride and self-worth that boosts self-esteem.

3. Reduced cravings – Celebrating milestones provides a distraction from cravings and withdrawal symptoms associated with quitting smoking.

4. Improved mental health – Celebrating accomplishments reduces anxiety and depression associated with quitting smoking.

5. Improved physical health – Quitting smoking improves physical health, and celebrating milestones is a sure way of staying on track and enjoying a healthier life.

Conclusion

Quitting smoking is a journey, and celebrating milestones and accomplishments is a crucial aspect of enhancing the chances of success. Celebrating milestones provides motivation, boosts self-esteem, reduces cravings, and improves mental and physical health. The journey to quit smoking requires discipline, determination, and the right support methods. There are various approaches to quitting smoking, and the choice depends on the individual. Cold turkey, nicotine replacement therapy, prescription medications, behavioral therapy, and support groups are some of the approaches that people use to quit smoking. Celebrating milestones can be done in various ways, including creating a quit plan, reward system, sharing success stories, setting up a savings account, and keeping a journal. Quitting smoking is not easy, but with the right approach and support, people can lead a healthier and fulfilling life.

5. Quiz

1. What is an effective method to help you stay smoke-free?

a) Replace cigarettes with nicotine gum
   b) Avoid situations that trigger cravings
   c) Reduce daily smoking instead of quitting cold turkey
   d) Engage in activities that distract you from thinking about smoking

2. What should you do if you have a relapse and smoke a cigarette?

a) Give up on quitting and continue smoking
   b) Punish yourself for relapsing
   c) Remind yourself of your reasons for quitting and continue working towards being smoke-free
   d) Smoke a couple of cigarettes to relieve the craving and then quit again

3. What can help reduce the intensity of cravings and withdrawal symptoms?

a) Drinking alcohol
   b) Eating high-sugar snacks
   c) Staying hydrated and eating a balanced diet
   d) Avoiding exercise

4. What is a common trigger for smoking cravings?

a) Stress
   b) Eating a large meal
   c) Watching TV
   d) Drinking water

5. How can you reward yourself for staying smoke-free?

a) Buy a pack of cigarettes
   b) Go out to a fancy dinner
   c) Exercise or engage in a fun activity
   d) Take a day off work

Answers:

1. b) Avoid situations that trigger cravings
   2. c) Remind yourself of your reasons for quitting and continue working towards being smoke-free
   3. c) Staying hydrated and eating a balanced diet
   4. a) Stress
   5. c) Exercise or engage in a fun activity

VIII. Helping Others Quit

1. Strategies for supporting loved ones

Introduction

Smoking cessation, or quitting smoking, can be challenging as it is not only a physical addiction to nicotine but it is also a habit that involves emotional and social factors. It is not uncommon for individuals attempting to quit smoking to have periods of relapse. Therefore, it can be helpful for loved ones to provide support to those trying to quit smoking. In this essay, we will discuss several strategies for supporting loved ones in their journey to quit smoking.

1. Understanding the Importance of Quitting

One of the ways loved ones can support those trying to quit smoking is by understanding the importance of quitting. Although nicotine is highly addictive, not smoking is generally the best choice for overall physical health. Smoking is linked to a wide range of health issues, including lung cancer, heart disease, and chronic obstructive pulmonary disease (COPD). Therefore, knowledge of the detrimental health effects associated with smoking can motivate individuals to quit.

Additionally, smoking is expensive. According to the American Lung Association, the average cost of a pack of cigarettes is around $6.28, but this can vary depending on location. A person who smokes one pack a day will, therefore, spend around $189.84 a month or $2,278.08 per year. This knowledge may provide additional motivation for quitting smoking.

2. Encouraging a Healthy Lifestyle

A healthy lifestyle can decrease the desire to smoke cigarettes. Encouraging loved ones to make healthier choices, such as eating nutritious foods, engaging in regular exercise, and getting enough sleep, can help in the process of quitting smoking. Consuming foods that are rich in vitamins and antioxidants, such as fruits and vegetables, can provide a boost to the immune system, which can aid in the cessation process. Physical exercise also helps with stress relief, which is one of the main reasons individuals smoke. Getting enough rest ensures that the body is not fatigued, which can reduce the urge to smoke.

3. Creating a Support System

Creating a support system is essential for quitting smoking. Loved ones can be a significant part of this support system. Encouraging individuals to reach out to friends and family members who have either quit smoking or are currently going through the cessation process can be beneficial. This will help create a sense of community, which can help individuals feel less alone in the process.

Furthermore, loved ones can be a crucial part of support groups or other organized smoking cessation programs. Studies have shown that group therapy can be effective in helping individuals quit smoking. These groups provide a sense of belonging and can help individuals feel accountable for their actions.

4. Using Nicotine Replacements

Nicotine replacements can also be helpful in the process of quitting smoking. Nicotine replacement therapy (NRT) is designed to reduce the effects of nicotine withdrawal symptoms. This therapy works by replacing the nicotine in cigarettes with some other source of nicotine such as nicotine gum, patches, lozenges, or inhalers. These replacements are available over the counter or through prescription. However, it should be noted that NRT is still a nicotine-based product and should be used under the care of a healthcare professional.

5. Helping to Avoid Triggers

Avoiding triggers that may cause a relapse is an essential part of the cessation process. Triggers can vary from individual to individual and can include specific people, locations, or experiences. For instance, certain people in the individual's life may trigger the desire to smoke cigarettes. Those who may trigger the individual should be avoided or limited in contact.

Likewise, certain locations or experiences can also be triggers for smoking. Examples of such triggers include parties where other attendees are smoking, or a stressful situation that may cause an individual to crave cigarettes. Avoiding such scenarios may help prevent relapses.

6. Motivating and Uplifting

Finally, loved ones should strive to be motivational and uplifting to individuals trying to quit smoking. Quitting smoking is not an easy process. It can be physically and emotionally draining. Therefore, individuals attempting to quit smoking should be surrounded by positive individuals who are supportive of their efforts. It is essential to encourage them to keep going during difficult times.

Conclusion

In conclusion, support from loved ones is crucial for individuals going through the process of quitting smoking. Strategies such as understanding the importance of quitting, encouraging a healthy lifestyle, creating a support system, using nicotine replacements, helping to avoid triggers, and being motivational and uplifting can help individuals in their journey to quit smoking. Understanding that quitting smoking is a challenging process is essential, and providing support as well as a sense of accountability is key. Loved ones must be supportive, non-judgmental, and understanding throughout the process.

2. Encouraging and motivating others to quit

Introduction

Smoking is a notorious habit that affects the health and wellbeing of a significant number of individuals worldwide. Research indicates that smoking leads to various chronic diseases, including heart disease, lung cancer, and respiratory complications. Despite the health implications, quitting smoking can be a challenging task for most individuals. Nicotine, a highly addictive substance in cigarettes, makes it hard for smokers to quit the habit. Fortunately, there are various ways to encourage and motivate smokers to quit. This paper explores six effective approaches to inspire and motivate others to quit smoking.

Lead By Example

One of the best ways of encouraging smokers to quit is by leading by example. Non-smokers who surround smokers should avoid smoking or using tobacco products. By doing so, the smokers may get encouraged to quit, knowing that it is possible to live without cigarettes. Quitting smoking can be a daunting task; however, it is possible to achieve. Non-smokers can showcase how happy, and healthy living without smoking can be. Additionally, non-smokers can highlight the positive impacts quitting smoking has on their lives. Smokers may become more motivated to quit smoking once they see the benefits of living smoke-free.

Provide Support

Support is a vital component when it comes to quitting smoking. The support offered to individuals who want to quit smoking increases their chances of quitting and remaining smoke-free. Family, friends, and colleagues can offer to support smokers by calling them regularly, sending text messages, and encouraging them to keep going. Smokers going through withdrawal symptoms or struggling with addiction may also need professional support. Healthcare providers can provide medical assistance, such as the prescription of nicotine replacement therapy to reduce cravings and manage withdrawal symptoms.

Encourage the Use of Nicotine Replacement Therapy

Nicotine replacement therapy (NRT) is a treatment option that provides smokers with nicotine in smaller doses than cigarettes. The therapy helps in managing the uncomfortable symptoms that arise during nicotine withdrawal. Examples of nicotine replacement therapy products include nicotine gums, lozenges, inhalers, and patches. The use of nicotine replacement therapy can enhance the smoker's chances of quitting, especially if used in combination with other quitting methods. Family members, friends, and healthcare providers can offer guidance to smokers on choosing and using the appropriate nicotine product to help them quit smoking.

Provide Information on the Health Risks Associated with Smoking

Smokers often underestimate the health risks associated with smoking. It is essential to inform smokers about the health implications of smoking and the benefits of quitting. Informing smokers about the long-term effects of smoking on their health may motivate them to quit. These effects include an increased risk of heart disease, stroke, respiratory complications, and various types of cancer. Smokers may also experience reduced physical fitness, reduced lung capacity, premature skin aging, and yellowing of teeth and fingernails. Family members and friends can provide smokers with information on the advantages of quitting and the negative outcomes of not quitting.

Provide Distractions

Distractions can help smokers to deal with cravings, and avoid the urge to smoke. Family, friends, and coworkers can suggest activities that may help distract smokers, such as going for a walk, engaging in sports or physical activities, or reading a book. Distractions can engage smokers in activities that divert their attention from smoking, help the time pass, and ease the withdrawal symptoms. Learning new hobbies, acquiring new skills or participating in community activities may also help distract the smoker from smoking.

Encourage and offer positive reinforcement

Offering positive reinforcement can encourage smokers to keep going, and help them overcome the challenges of quitting. Family members, friends, and coworkers can praise smokers for their efforts towards quitting, regardless of their progress. Rewarding smokers for milestones achieved can boost their motivation to continue the quitting journey. For instance, rewarding a smoker for going a day smoke-free, a week smoke-free, or a month smoke-free can give them the morale to keep going. Positive reinforcement creates a sense of accomplishment, and smokers are more likely to remain motivated towards quitting.

Conclusion

Quitting smoking is a difficult journey, and smokers may need various forms of support and motivation to help them overcome the habit. Advising friends and loved ones to quit smoking can positively impact their wellbeing and improve the health of the entire community. Encouraging smokers to lead by example, provide support, use nicotine replacement therapy, provide distractions, offer information on the health risks, and offering positive reinforcement are effective ways of motivating smokers to quit. It is possible to quit smoking, and every smoker deserves the opportunity to experience the benefits of a life without cigarettes.

3. Resources for friends and family of smokers

Introduction

Smoking is a prevalent and harmful habit that affects both smokers and those around them. It is a leading cause of death and a significant contributor to various medical conditions such as cancer, heart diseases, and respiratory ailments. Quitting smoking is a challenging process that requires support and motivation from family and friends. Often, smokers find it hard to quit on their own, and therefore, seek help from their loved ones. As a friend or family member of a smoker, it's essential to be prepared to offer support and resources. This paper delves into resources for friends and family of smokers on how to stop smoking.

The health risks of smoking

Smoking poses significant health risks to the smoker and those around them. It is the leading cause of preventable death, with more than seven million people dying globally each year. Apart from causing cancer, smoking also increases the risk of heart diseases, respiratory conditions, and stroke. Furthermore, it contributes to premature aging, poor oral health, and fertility problems. Secondhand smoking is equally harmful to others, leading to lung-related complications such as asthma and pneumonia, ear infections, and sudden infant death syndrome in children.

Ways to Quit Smoking

Quitting smoking is not an easy process and requires a combination of strategies and resources such as counseling, medication, and support from family and friends. The following are some of the common ways to quit smoking:

Nicotine Replacement Therapy (NRT): This strategy involves replacing the nicotine in cigarettes with a low dose of nicotine through patches, gums, or lozenges. NRT helps to ease the nicotine withdrawal symptoms and cravings.

Behavioral Therapy: It is a psychological treatment that helps smokers to identify and avoid triggers that make them smoke. Counseling and support groups such as Nicotine Anonymous help smokers to learn coping mechanisms and alternate ways of handling stress.

Prescription Medications: There are prescription drugs such as Zyban and Chantix that help to reduce the cravings for nicotine.

Cold Turkey: This involves quitting smoking without the aid of medication or therapy. It is the most challenging and commonly fails when not coupled with other strategies.

Resources for Friends and Family of Smokers

As friends or family members of a smoker, it's essential to provide support and resources to help them quit smoking successfully. The following are some of the resources that can be helpful:

1. Educational Resources: Friends and family can arm themselves with knowledge of the dangers of smoking, the benefits of quitting, and strategies for quitting.

The National Cancer Institute: They have various educational resources that provide information on the health risks of smoking, strategies to quit smoking, and support resources such as a quitline (1-877-44U-QUIT).

The American Cancer Society: They offer educational resources, tools, and support for smokers and their loved ones. They have a 24-hour helpline (1-800-227-2345) and online chat services that smokers can use to get support.

2. Quitline Services: Quitline services are free, convenient, and offer confidential support for those seeking to quit smoking. They provide resources and support via phone or chat services.

The National Quitline: This is a federally funded service that provides free support, resources, and counseling services to smokers who want to quit. The National Quitline (1-800-QUIT-NOW) offers help in English and Spanish.

Local Quitlines: Most states have their Quitlines that offer free services to smokers who want to quit. The local Quitlines provide personalized counseling and referrals to local resources.

3. Support Groups: Support groups provide a safe space for smokers to share their experiences, challenges, and successes in quitting smoking. They offer emotional support, guidance, and camaraderie essential for successful quitting.

Nicotine Anonymous: It is a support group based on the principles of Alcoholics Anonymous that offer support, guidance, and encouragement to smokers seeking to quit.

Smokefree.gov: They offer free online support groups and live chat sessions that provide smokers with guidance, resources, and strategies for successful quitting.

4. Apps & Online Programs: There are several apps and online programs that provide personalized support, monitoring, and tools to help smokers quit.

Quit Genius: It is a personalized online program that offers tailored support, coaching, and behavior therapy to help smokers quit smoking.

Become an Ex: It is a free online program that provides daily support, advice, information, and tools to help smokers quit smoking.

5. Medications and Therapy: As friends or family members, you can help smokers by providing financial support for medication, therapy, or counseling. The following resources can be helpful:

Rx Outreach: It is a non-profit organization that provides affordable medications to low-income families, including smoking cessation drugs.

Behavioral Therapy: Offer to accompany smokers to therapy or counseling sessions to provide them with the necessary emotional support.

Conclusion

Quitting smoking is a challenging process that requires support, motivation, and resources. As friends and family members, it's crucial to offer smokers the necessary support and resources to help them quit successfully. Educational resources, quitline services, support groups, apps, online programs, and medication therapy are all resources that can be helpful in the quitting process. Supporting smokers in their quitting journey can help reduce the number of smoking-related deaths and improve the quality of life for smokers and others around them.

4. Quiz

1. Which of the following is NOT a benefit of quitting smoking?

a. Decreased risk of heart disease
   b. Improved lung function
   c. Increased risk of cancer
   d. Improved sense of taste and smell

Answer: c. Increased risk of cancer

2. What is the most effective way to help someone quit smoking?

a. Lecture them about the dangers of smoking
   b. Nag them to quit constantly
   c. Offer support and encouragement
   d. Smoke around them to make them uncomfortable

Answer: c. Offer support and encouragement

3. Why is it important to have open, honest communication with someone trying to quit smoking?

a. It allows them to vent their frustrations and fears

b. It helps them feel supported and less alone

c. It can help identify triggers for smoking and develop coping strategies

d. All of the above

Answer: d. All of the above

4. What are some alternative activities or habits that can replace smoking?

a. Exercise

b. Chewing gum

c. Deep breathing exercises

d. All of the above

Answer: d. All of the above

5. How long does it typically take for the withdrawal symptoms of nicotine to subside?

a. 1-2 days

b. 1-2 weeks

c. 1-2 months

d. 1-2 years

Answer: b. 1-2 weeks

IX. Conclusion

1. Recap of the importance of quitting smoking

Introduction

Cigarette smoking is one of the leading causes of death in the world today. Smoking has many negative effects on the body, including lung cancer, heart disease, and respiratory problems. Many people struggle with quitting smoking, but it is a vital step for improving health and decreasing the risk of cancer and other smoking-related diseases. This paper aims to recap the importance of quitting smoking in relation to How to Stop Smoking.

Importance of Quitting Smoking

Quitting smoking has many benefits for the body, including the following:

1. Reduced Risk of Cancer

Smoking is a significant cause of many types of cancer, including lung, throat, mouth, and bladder cancer. Quitting smoking reduces the risk of developing these types of cancer.

2. Improved Lung Function

Smoking damages the lungs and decreases lung function. Quitting smoking can improve lung function and reduce the risk of lung-related diseases such as chronic obstructive pulmonary disease (COPD).

3. Improved Heart Health

Smoking increases the risk of heart disease. Quitting smoking can improve heart health and reduce the risk of heart attacks and strokes.

4. Increased Life Expectancy

Smokers have a shorter life expectancy than nonsmokers. Quitting smoking can increase life expectancy and improve overall health.

How to Stop Smoking

There are many ways to stop smoking, including the following:

1. Cold Turkey

Cold turkey is the process of quitting smoking abruptly without the aid of nicotine replacement therapy (NRT) or other cessation aids. It can be challenging to quit smoking cold turkey, but it is an effective method for some people.

2. Nicotine Replacement Therapy

Nicotine replacement therapy (NRT) involves using products such as gum, patches, lozenges, or inhalers that provide a source of nicotine without the harmful additives found in cigarettes. NRT can help reduce withdrawal symptoms and cravings, making it easier to stop smoking.

3. Prescription Medications

There are prescription medications available that can help people quit smoking. These medications work by reducing the urge to smoke and reducing withdrawal symptoms. Examples of prescription medications include bupropion (Zyban) and varenicline (Chantix).

4. Behavioral Therapy

Behavioral therapy can help people quit smoking by providing support and teaching coping skills to deal with cravings and triggers. Behavioral therapy can be conducted individually or in a group setting.

Conclusion

Quitting smoking is a vital step for improving health and reducing the risk of cancer and other smoking-related diseases. There are many ways to stop smoking, including cold turkey, nicotine replacement therapy, prescription medications, and behavioral therapy. Although it can be challenging to quit smoking, it is worth the effort to improve overall health and increase life expectancy.

2. Encouragement for readers to take action

Introduction

Smoking is a harmful and addictive habit that affects millions of people worldwide. According to the World Health Organization (WHO), smoking is responsible for around six million deaths every year, and it is estimated that half of the world's population will die prematurely due to smoking-related illnesses. Despite these grim statistics, quitting smoking is not an easy task. It requires a great deal of effort, commitment, and support. In this essay, I will discuss the importance of taking action to quit smoking, the reasons why people find it difficult to quit, and some practical tips for quitting.

The Importance of Taking Action to Quit Smoking

Quitting smoking is one of the most important things you can do for your health. Smoking damages every organ in the body and increases the risk of numerous diseases, including lung cancer, heart disease, stroke, and respiratory illnesses. It also affects the people around you, as exposure to secondhand smoke can cause health problems in non-smokers, especially children.

Quitting smoking can be challenging, but taking action to quit is crucial for your health. Smoking cessation not only reduces your risk of developing smoking-related illnesses, but it can also improve your quality of life. According to the American Lung Association, quitting smoking can lead to immediate health benefits, such as improved circulation, increased lung function, and reduced risk of infections. Long-term benefits of quitting smoking include a reduced risk of heart attack, stroke, and lung cancer.

Reasons Why People Find it Difficult to Quit Smoking

Despite the many health benefits of quitting smoking, many people find it difficult to quit. Nicotine, the addictive substance in cigarettes, makes quitting smoking challenging. Nicotine triggers the release of dopamine in the brain, which creates a pleasurable sensation. Over time, the brain becomes dependent on nicotine to produce this pleasurable feeling, which leads to cravings and withdrawal symptoms when nicotine is not present in the body.

In addition to nicotine addiction, several other factors can make quitting smoking difficult. Smoking can be a social habit, and smokers may feel pressure from friends or family members who smoke. Stress, anxiety, and depression can also trigger cravings for cigarettes, making it hard to quit smoking.

Practical Tips for Quitting Smoking

Quitting smoking is not easy, but it is achievable with the right tools and support. Here are some practical tips for quitting smoking:

1. Make a plan: Decide on a quit date and stick to it. Make a plan for how you will cope with cravings and withdrawal symptoms.

2. Get support: Tell your friends and family members that you are quitting smoking and ask for their support. Consider joining a support group or seeking professional help.

3. Use nicotine replacement therapy: Nicotine replacement therapy, such as nicotine patches or gum, can help reduce cravings and withdrawal symptoms.

4. Avoid triggers: Identify what triggers your cravings and try to avoid these triggers as much as possible. For example, if you usually smoke when you drink coffee, switch to tea for a while.

5. Exercise: Regular exercise can help reduce stress and anxiety, which can trigger cravings for cigarettes.

6. Practice mindfulness: Mindfulness techniques, such as meditation and deep breathing, can help you cope with cravings and reduce stress.

Conclusion

Quitting smoking is one of the most important steps you can take to improve your health and well-being. Although quitting smoking can be challenging, it is achievable with the right tools and support. By making a plan, getting support, using nicotine replacement therapy, avoiding triggers, exercising, and practicing mindfulness, you can increase your chances of quitting smoking successfully. Remember that quitting smoking is a process, and it may take several attempts before you succeed. Keep trying, and don't give up. The benefits of quitting smoking are worth the effort.

3. Quiz

1. What is the best way to stop smoking?
    a) Going cold turkey
    b) Using nicotine replacement therapy
    c) Joining a support group
    d) Combining all three methods

2. What is the ultimate goal of quitting smoking?
    a) Reducing the risks of health problems
    b) Saving money
    c) Improving personal relationships
    d) All of the above

3. What can happen if you do not quit smoking?
    a) Increased risk of cancer
    b) Poor circulation
    c) Heart disease
    d) All of the above

4. What are common withdrawal symptoms when quitting smoking?
    a) Cravings
    b) Irritability
    c) Difficulty concentrating
    d) All of the above

5. What can be helpful in managing withdrawal symptoms?

a) Deep breathing exercises
b) Staying hydrated
c) Engaging in physical activity
d) All of the above

6. What is the importance of a support system when quitting smoking?
    a) It provides accountability
    b) It offers emotional support
    c) It provides motivation
    d) All of the above

7. What is the long-term benefit of quitting smoking?
    a) Increased life expectancy
    b) Reduced risk of health problems
    c) Improved financial situation
    d) All of the above

8. What can trigger a desire to smoke?
    a) Stress
    b) Social situations
    c) Alcohol consumption
    d) All of the above

9. What can be helpful in avoiding triggers?
    a) Avoiding certain situations
    b) Finding alternative coping mechanisms
    c) Creating a plan
    d) All of the above

10. What is the biggest takeaway from learning about how to stop smoking?

    a) Quitting smoking is a difficult but achievable goal

    b) There are various methods and resources available to assist

    c) The benefits of quitting outweigh the potential struggles

    d) All of the above

Ingram Content Group UK Ltd.
Milton Keynes UK
UKHW010854060623
422954UK00001B/105